THE REVENUE RESOURCES OF THE MUGHAL EMPIRE IN INDIA

THE REVENUE RESOURCES OF THE MUGHAL EMPIRE IN INDIA

FROM
A.D. 1593 TO A.D. 1707:

A SUPPLEMENT TO THE CHRONICLES OF THE PATHÀN KINGS OF DEHLI

EDWARD THOMAS

GYAN

Published by

Gyan Publishing House
5, Ansari Road
Daryaganj, New Delhi-110002
Phone: 011-47034999, 9811692060
E-mail: books@gyanbooks.com

Distribution Network
gyanbooks.com
India, USA, Canada, UK, Australia

ISBN: 978-93-7225-215-6 (HB)

First Published, 1871

2nd Impression 2025

Printed at: Gyan Press, Delhi.

THE REVENUE RESOURCES OF THE MUGHAL EMPIRE IN INDIA

Author: EDWARD THOMAS

THE REVENUE RESOURCES OF THE MUGHAL EMPIRE IN INDIA,

FROM A.D. 1593 TO A.D. 1707.

A SUPPLEMENT

TO

THE CHRONICLES OF THE PATHÁN KINGS OF DEHLI.

BY

EDWARD THOMAS, F.R.S.,

LATE OF THE EAST INDIA COMPANY'S BENGAL CIVIL SERVICE.

LONDON:

TRÜBNER & CO., 8 AND 60, PATERNOSTER ROW.

1871.

PREFACE.

The subjoined compilation embraces much new matter, which was necessarily omitted from the brief Appendix on the Revenues of the Mughals, inserted in my late work on "The Pathán Kings of Dehli."

The growing interest of the subject, and the surprise expressed at the amounts realized at these periods, have induced me to scrutinize more fully the available data, and to present them in the amplified form of a Supplement to the "Chronicles" of the race, whose defeat secured the dominion of the Mughal.

London,
November, 1871.

REVENUES OF THE MUGHAL EMPIRE.

FÍRÚZ SHÁH'S REVENUES.

I HAVE had occasion to advert in the pages of "The Chronicles of the Pathán Kings of Dehli," to the revenues of India under Akbar, in elucidation of the State resources of his predecessors. As much difficulty has hitherto been felt in the definition of values, even where figures were unassailable, I revert to the subject as an appropriate sequel to Akbar's monetary system, in order to exhibit more fully, by absolute numismatic data, the intrinsic amount of the taxes imposed. And, further, in consideration of the interest at present attaching to the question of British Indian finance, I have taken advantage of this opportunity to extend my previous notice to an examination of the revenues of the later Mughal monarchs, so as to place before the public a progressive series of Imperial balance sheets extending up to 1707 A.D., when our own countrymen began to appear in force upon the Húghli, when Job Charnock, "the father of Calcutta," was buried in his own city (1692), and the foundation of "Fort William, in Bengal," (1700), foreshadowed the reduction of Agrah, Dehli, and Láhor to provincial capitals.

Before entering upon the details of Akbar's revenue, it may be as well to dispose of the earlier returns of Fírúz Sháh and Bábar, which in their modest totals only confuse the sequence of the Mughal lists, and in reality have little or no bearing upon the State resources of the later periods, which were derived from so much more extended an empire. Fírúz Sháh's revenue in A.D. 1351–1388 is fixed at £6,850,000, and that of Bábar in A.D. 1526–1530 at £2,600,000.[1]

The contrast of the relatively large income of Fírúz Sháh, with his avowedly narrowed boundaries, would naturally seem to conflict with the reduced total confessed to by Bábar, who boasted of so much greater a breadth of territory; but these difficulties are susceptible of various simple explanations. In Fírúz Sháh's forty years of undisturbed repose, the country was positively full to overflowing of the precious metals, which had been uniformly attracted towards the capital from various causes for nearly a century previously. The bullion resources of the metropolitan provinces may be tested by the multitude of the extant specimens of the gold and silver coinages of the previous reigns, and the confessed facility with which millions might be accumulated by officials of no very high degree. The whole land was otherwise teeming with material wealth, and was administered by Hindú *vazírs* and other home-taught men, who realized every fraction that the State could claim.

Far different were the circumstances which Bábar's limited tenure of his straggling conquests presented. Tímúr had already effectually ruined the land through which his plundering hordes had passed—what his followers could not carry away they destroyed; and while the distant provinces retained their metallic stores, the old capital and all around it was impoverished to desolation; so that when the prestige of Dehli re-asserted itself under Buhlól Lódi, he was forced to resort to the indigenous copper mines for a new currency

1 See "Chronicles of the Pathán Kings," p. 272, note (the figures for Fírúz's revenues in Sir H. Elliot's Historians, vol. iii. p. 288, are partially corrected at p. 346 of the same volume, where the *written* sum is 6,85,00,000 *tankahs*). Bábar's returns are given at p. 388 of my work.

("Chronicles," p. 361); and though public affairs and national prosperity improved under his son Sikandar, the standard coin was only raised to something like $\frac{1}{10}$ silver to the copper basis, which, however, secured a more portable piece, and a more creditable value, in a currency which found ready acceptance with races who had already been educated in the theory of mixed metals. The substantial development of Hindústán under Ibrahím, the son of Sikandar, was absolutely unprecedented. Cheapness and plenty became fabulous even to the native mind, but this very prosperity of the people reduced, *pari passu*, the income of the king, which was derived directly from the produce of the land, his dues being payable in kind; so that when corn was cheap the money value of his revenues declined in nearly equal proportion.[1] And thus it came about that when Bábar examined the accumulated treasures of the house of Lódi, on the capture of Agrah, he found but little beyond the current copper coinage, leavened, as it was, with a small modicum of silver.

The statistical returns of Bábar's time were clearly based upon the old rent-rolls of that unacknowledged contributor to the efficiency of all later Indian revenue systems, Sikandar bin Buhlól. A single subdued confession in Bábar's table[2]

[1] It was with a view to remedy this state of things that Akbar introduced his *ten* years' settlement, the germ of that pernicious measure, Lord Cornwallis's notable Perpetual Settlement. Akbar's intentions were equitable, and, to his perceptions, the enforced pact as between king and subject left little to be objected to; but the uniformity it was desired to promote was dependent upon higher powers, and the Indian climate could not be made a party to the treaty. Hence, in bad seasons, the arrangement worked harshly against the poorer husbandmen, and threw them more and more into the hands of usurers, whose lawful Oriental rate of interest was enough to crush far more thrifty cultivators than the ordinary Indian *Raiyat*. The *ten* years' settlement itself was based upon the average returns of the ten preceding harvests, from the fifteenth to the twenty-fourth year (inclusive) of Akbar's reign (Gladwin, i. p. 366).

[2] No. 5, "Méwát, not included in Sikandar's revenue roll" (Chronicles, p. 390).

suffices to prove this, and simultaneously with the retention of these State ledgers the interlopers clearly accepted the official method of reckoning in Sikandari Tankahs, which, numismatically speaking, must have been almost the only coins available at the period, the profuse issue of which may be tested by the multitude of the pieces still in existence, and the completeness of the series of dates spreading over twenty-six continuous years of Sikandar's reign, already cited at page 366 of the "Chronicles."

But perhaps the most simple way of reconciling the striking discrepancy between the two sums assigned severally as the Imperial dues under Fírúz and Bábar, would be to suppose that the comparatively large amount of the revenue of the former monarch comprehended within its terms income from all sources, while the reduced estimate of Bábar's chronicler may be held to refer to the State demand upon the land alone, which the conqueror was able directly to enforce from the recorded assessments of the previous reign. The incidental statements of Fírúz Sháh's special biographer, quoted at p. 272, give countenance to such an inference, especially in the item of the £300,000 of vexatious taxes abandoned by Fírúz in A.H. 777 (A.D. 1375-6),[1] and the general terms in which the total income is adverted to.

[1] It is seldom we find an Oriental potentate testifying, under his own hand, to the iniquities of no less than twenty-four taxes he had previously tacitly sanctioned, and whose abolition he not only frankly proclaims in his own autobiography, but whose perpetual extinction was supposed to be secured by the display of this same royal manifesto on the surface of the walls of the Mosque he had founded for the good of his own soul, in his new capital on the banks of the Jumna ("Chronicles," p. 289, note 2); and yet so readily did the authorities fall back upon those ancient imposts, that we find many of the same items entered in the new relinquishment of oppressive demands under Akbar (pp. 17-19, *infrà*). The list of curious cesses given by Fírúz Sháh, so suggestive of a primitive stage of civilization, is here subjoined, together with the far more important declaration,

AKBAR'S REVENUES.

The earliest and probably the most competent and trustworthy author who furnishes any return of Akbar's revenue is Nizám-ud-dín Ahmad, a, so to say, practised accountant,

on the part of the reigning monarch, of the specific taxes he was content to recognize as the Royal demand, in full, against all classes of his subjects.

LIST OF IMPOSTS PROFESSEDLY ABOLISHED BY FÍRÚZ SHÁH IN A.D. 1375.

1. مندوي برگ Market dues.
2. دلالت بازارها Brokerage. (No. 35 of Akbar's list, p. 19.)
3. جزاري Slaughter-houses. (12 *jítals* for every ox, etc. No. 22 of Akbar's list.)
4. اميري طرب Leaders of music and dancing. (Nautches?)
5. گلفروشي Perfumery.
6. "حرينه" تنبول Betel.
7. چنگي غله Octroi (*lit.* handfuls of grain taken, in kind, as town dues), a tax still wisely conceded to the home instincts of our native townships in the Punjáb.
8. كتابي Books.
9. نيلكري Indigo. (Dyes, No. 37?)
10. ماهي فروشي Fish. (No. 36.)
11. ندافي Cotton-cleaning.
12. صابونكري Soap-manufacture.
13. ريسمان فروشي Silk.
14. روغن كري *Ghí* (clarified butter). (No. 18.)
15. نخود بريان Parched grain.
16. ته بازاري Ground rent of stalls in the market. (ته fold, stratum.)
17. حهبه [چبپه for *Chhâp*, synonymous with *Chânk*, a stamp set upon stacks, under *Batâí* tenures].
18. قمارخانه Gambling-houses. (No. 24.)
19. دادبنكي (बनियाक) Fees to heads of trades (Chaudharís).
20. كوتوالي Fees to Kotwáls. (No. 8.)

and a most experienced revenue administrator, who describes a condition of things of which he had the fullest means of official knowledge.[1] I repeat the substance, and enlarge the

21. احتسابي Inspectors of markets.
22. كرهي (Sansk. गृह, Hind. घर) House tax.
23. چرائي Pasture dues.
24. مصادرات Fines and amercements.

TAXES SPECIALLY AUTHORIZED BY FÍRÚZ ON HIS OWN INTERPRETATION OF THE KURÁN.

1. خراج اراضي عشور $\frac{1}{10}$ on cultivated land.
2. زكوة Alms, or a "poor rate, the portion or amount of property that is given therefrom, as the due of God, to the poor." Usually assessed at $\frac{1}{40}$, or $2\frac{1}{2}$ per cent. (Lane.)
3. جزية هنود Capitation tax on Hindús (three grades, @ 40, 20, and 10 *tankahs*).
4. (تَرِكَة) تركات. Res relicta), the *Ldwdris mdl* of the present day. The *Wala Imdmat* of the Western interpreters, *i.e.* "Inheritance of dominion," or heritage of the head of the State.
5. خمس غنايم ومعادن. $\frac{1}{5}$ of all spoils and produce of mines.

—From the Persian MS. فتوحات فيروزشاهي.

Shams-i-Siráj 'Afíf, Fírúz's especial biographer, also adverts to this abolition of oppressive taxes; he notices as specially objectionable—1st. The system of demanding extra fees, entitled *Ddngdna* (or one *ddng* in the *tankah*), in addition to the authorized *Zakdt*, exacted on the entry of merchandize into towns. 2nd. The مشتغل *Mushtaghal* or كرا زمين *Kird-i-zamín*, "ground rent" (?) on the shops and houses of Dehli, which amounted to as much as 1,50,000 *tankahs* per annum. 3rd. The جزاري mentioned in Fírúz Sháh's list (No. 3). 4th. The روزي *Rozi*, or one day's labour exacted by the officials from every beast of burden entering the town with merchandize. The author concludes by noticing that this edict of Fírúz Sháh's was proclaimed in his presence, in A.H. 777, and that the consequent loss to the State was estimated at 30,00,000 *tankahs* (£300,000). See Professor Dowson's translation, Elliot's Historians, iii. pp. 363–6, 377; Briggs's Ferishtah, i. p. 463; Ferishtah, Bombay Persian text, i. p. 272.

[1] See "Chronicles," p. 388. This is not the place to enlarge upon the merits of the author of the Tabakát-i Akbari (otherwise known as the Táríkh-i Nizámi). Suffice it to say, that Nizám-ud-dín Ahmad, with his father's rank to recommend

context, of the passage quoted at p. 388 of the "Chronicles," giving his statement of the amount of the current income. Speaking of the country of Hindústán, he proceeds—"Its length from Hindú Kóh, on the borders of Badakhshán, to the country of Orissa, which is on the borders of Bengal, from west to east, is 1680 legal *kos*. Its breadth from Kashmír to the hills of Barújh, which is on the borders of Súrat and Gujarát, is 800 *kos* Iláhi. Another mode is to take the breadth from the hills of Kumáon to the borders of the Dakhan, which amounts to 1000 Iláhi *kos*. . . . At the present time, namely A.H. 1002,[1] Hindústán contains 3200 towns, (including 120 large cities) and 500,000 villages, and yields a revenue of 640,00,00,000 *tankah Murádi*." The writer adds, that as there is no room for the list of cities in this summary, he proposes to give them in full alphabetical order on some future occasion, a task he was never able to fulfil, as he died in the same year.

There can be very little contest about the value of Nizám-ud-dín's pieces designated as "*Tankah Murádi*." They were in effect the old Sikandari Tankah of twenty to the *Silver Tankah* or Rupee, of which numerous proofs have already been adduced.[2] So that the total revenue of the kingdom is here defined as £32,000,000.[3] It is not expressly stated whether

him, secured, in early life, a position at the Court of Akbar; and in that monarch's twenty-ninth year attained the dignity of *Bakhshi* of Gujarát. The value of his work has been freely testified to by *Budaoni* (a contemporary author of nearly equal credit), in his declaration, that "Nizám-ud-dín Ahmad spent his life in the service of the Emperor Akbar, (and) his history in all that relates to the reign of that Sovereign can be implicitly relied upon." Elliot's Index, p. 204; Morley's Catalogue of the Royal Asiatic Society's MSS., p. 61; Stewart's Catalogue of Tippoo Sultán's Library, p. 11; Col. N. Lees, Journal Royal Asiatic Society, vol. iii., N.S., p. 458.

[1] A.H. 1002 commenced on the 17th of September, 1593.

[2] "Chronicles," pp. 336, 370, 384, 387, 437.

[3] 640,00,00,000 ÷ 20 = 32,00,00,000 ÷ 10 = £32,000,000.

this sum is the produce of land revenue pure and simple, or the grand total of taxes, cesses and imposts of every description realized for the Imperial exchequer; but the latter seems to be the most reasonable conclusion, more especially as throughout these returns there will be found a closely relative proportion between the land revenue and the total income of the State from all sources, which latter rules more or less equably at double the former.

The Institutes of the Emperor Akbar embody a very complete description of the Indian revenue system, embracing the theory of assessment, methods of collection, and the general practical working of the indigenous scheme as matured by Shír Sháh; together with the tentative reforms introduced by Akbar's own ministers, so effectively completed by that paragon of Hindú *vazírs*, Rája Todar Mall.[1]

In cursorily noticing the leading peculiarities of the Indian land-tax, it may be as well to premise that the context of the Á'ín-i Akbari gives no countenance to the fiction of the State ownership of the soil,[2] the king's demand in no case extends beyond his share of the produce. It is true that an absolute monarch, who could take, with impunity, a subject's head, could with equal licence take that subject's land; but the

[1] Rája Todar Mall (Toral Mall) was not less brave as a soldier, and successful as a commander, than he was efficient as an administrator. His first prominent employment in the latter department was his assessment of Gujarát in the eighteenth year of Akbar's reign. In the twenty-second year he was made *vazír*, and in the twenty-seventh year he introduced his important financial reforms, associated with a complete change of the language in use in the revenue accounts, superseding the indigenous Hindí by the exotic Persian. Todar Mall died in A.H. 998.—Blochmann's Á'ín-i Akbari.

[2] By Muhammadan law, the Sovereign was only entitled to the regular one-fifth of the land taken in war (immovable possessions followed the same law as movable goods); he had, however, the option of taking that *fifth* as divided off land, or in one-fifth of the annual produce of the whole capture.—Sale's Kurán, i. p. 195.

soil was valueless without the *ascripti glebæ;* and so far from desiring to oust owners or occupiers, the *raiyat* was encouraged in every possible way to become a good cultivator. The king, in effect, was in partnership with the husbandmen of the nation: the more they succeeded in extracting from the earth, the more the Sovereign received as revenue; hence we find the ruling power using all kinds of devices to extend and improve the cultivation, commencing with advances to the needy, premiums upon the use of good seed, and other paternal measures, extending even to the despotic interdiction of the slaughter of "oxen, horses, buffaloes, or camels." [1]

The old system seems to have recognized nothing but payment in kind; and Akbar was so well aware of the advantage of such an arrangement to the agriculturists, that he invariably leaves the option of money payments to them, except in the case of sugar-cane, and such expensive crops, as implied the possession of certain means on the part of the grower, and a power to pay the State dues in cash. There were no less than four methods of estimating and setting apart the regal share of the produce which the occupier might elect to claim—1. The division of the field when sown; 2, an estimate on the standing crops; 3, a rough division by heaps; or 4, a precise division of grain. The introduction of the new settlement, which attempted to fix future payments on an average of the crops of the previous ten years, was calculated to act injuriously against the cultivator, in so far as it made no allowance for bad seasons, so that in extreme cases the poorer agriculturists might positively have to bor-

[1] Ibn Khordádbah mentions that the great Hajáj bin Yusaf, acting under the like crude idea, introduced a similar prohibition against the slaughter of oxen, very much to the disgust of the beef-eating population of Irák.—Journal Asiatique, 1865, p. 242.

row grain to meet the Government dues. With a notoriously improvident race, and money lenders who knew no usury laws, a single failure of the harvest might impoverish a village community for a generation; whereas, under the old system, the State shared the loss, and in famine-years could advance no claim whatever. If, in addition to these drawbacks, we take into consideration the fact that the Imperial demand ordinarily ranged at no less than one-third of the total crop,[1] it may be imagined how readily a confessedly fickle climate might disorganize the most elaborate calculations extending over far longer averages than any given *ten* years. The old system unquestionably insured a larger profit to the State in the long run,[2] and greater ease and comfort to the subject; while the new arrangement, sooner or later, must have involved reductions in the general average to secure uniformity and regularity of realization. No doubt, under the revised law, there were merciful considerations extended to defaulters; it was undesirable to kill the goose that laid the golden eggs; and the king's troops and the usurer alike understood that there were bold hearts and sharp swords in many an aboriginal village. The former were only employed in extreme cases, and the latter often had to risk something dearer than their own money.

Abúl Fazl's returns of Akbar's revenues are summarized from his imperfect data in the subjoined table, amounting, with later returns, but with all other deficiencies, to a total

[1] Akbar tells us that in former times the kings of India only took one-sixth of the produce. The rates of other Asiatic countries are specified. Turkey, one-fifth; Turán, one-sixth; Irán, one-tenth.—Áín-i Akbari, Gladwin, i. p. 349. (Shír Sháh claimed one-fourth.)

[2] A calculation has lately been made by a trustworthy writer in the *Calcutta Englishman* (August, 26, 1871), that if the province of Orissa had now to pay *in grain*, the Government would receive £1,000,000 instead of the £460,000 they compounded for in silver.

of *five arbs*,[1] *sixty-seven krors, sixty-three laks*, 83 *thousand and* 383 *dáms*, a sum not very far removed, with fair allowances for omissions in such imperfect documents,[2] from the speculative correction of *six arbs* (6,62,97,55,246), proposed at page 389 of the "Chronicles," an estimate I elsewhere adopt in preference to the tentative figures herein embodied, which were originally deduced simply for the purpose of testing my proposed emendation of Abúl Fazl's text, and which are now retained only for the purpose of instituting comparisons with the provincial statistics of subsequent reigns There is no suspicion of Abúl Fazl's want of faith, even if any motive could be imagined for such a tendency; but it is clear that a comprehensive work like the Áín-i Akbari, a positive gazetteer of all India, must have been compiled from the statistics of various State departments, working with little systematic concert, and its tabulated returns would at all times be liable to correction, as imperfectly brought up to the changes of the day.

It must be understood, in forming any comparative estimate of Akbar's assessments, that each province had to furnish a State contingent of cavalry and infantry, specified in full detail with other imperial demands, apart from the mere money payments entered in the divisional accounts; so that

[1] The *arb* अर्बुद ارب is 1000 millions, or 100 *krors*; the *kror* is 100 *laks*, and the *lak* 100 thousand. Wilson (Sanskrit Dictionary), Shakespeare (Hindustani Dictionary), and Haughton (Bengali Dictionary), alike concur in making the *arb* 100 millions; and the new St. Petersburgh Sanskrit Dictionary follows the same lead. Molesworth, in his Mahrattá Dictionary, however, gives "1000 millions," which the whole series of figures employed by the Muhammadan writers proves to be the correct amount. See also Elliot's Glossary, ii. p. 196.

[2] The majority of these *taḳsím jam'a* statements refer to the fifteenth year of the reign, and probably indicate a much lower revenue than the improved management of the succeeding twenty-five years secured for the State. The incorporation, however, of the returns of the new *ṣúbahs* plainly demonstrates the fact of later additions to the original text.

the country had to support a very large, though probably ineffective, army, over and above its ordinary revenue liabilities. The number of men mustered in this Zamíndári force is reckoned at the very high figure of 4,400,000,[1] in addition to the due proportion of horses and elephants each sub-division was bound to maintain. No reduction is, ostensibly, made in the State demand for the payment of these troops, who are styled بومی *Búmi*, "Landwehr," in contradistinction to the better organized Royal army. If we estimate the cost to the country for this force at the lowest possible figure of two rupees per man (including the purchase and feed of horses and elephants), it amounts of itself to a sum of more than ten millions of pounds, which as a purely speculative estimate might honestly be doubled.

		DÁMS.	RUPEES.
I.	Allahábád	21,24,27,119	53,10,677
II.	Agrah	[2] 54,62,50,304	1,36,56,257
III.	Oude	20,17,58,172	50,43,954
IV.	Ajmír	[3] 28,61,37,968	71,53,449
V.	Ahmadábád (Gujarát)	43,68,02,301	1,09,20,057
	" " Port dues	1,62,628	4,065
VI.	Bihár	22,19,19,404	55,47,985
VII.	Bengal	59,84,59,319	1,49,61,482
VIII.	Dehli	60,16,15,555	1,50,40,388
IX.	Kábul[4] { Simple *dáms*	27,27,17,786	
	Converted money (omitting payments in kind)	5,01,23,200	80,71,024
X.	Láhor	55,94,58,423	1,39,86,460

[1] Áín-i Akbari, text, p. 175; Gladwin's translation, p. 237.

[2] Gladwin has 64 *krors*.

[3] This total is obtained from the Sirkár details. Gladwin's text, p. 105, has only 2,28,41,507 *dáms*.

[4] Otherwise designated as "Ṣúbah Kashmír" (ii. p. 152), "Kábul, cited as the modern capital," (p. 199); in the final *taḳsím jam'a*, p. 107, however, it is described as "Ṣúbah Kábul." Under Sirkár Kandahár (p. 196), there is a full definition of the relative values of the coins, in which the comparative estimates

	DÁMS.	RUPEES.
XI. Multán	[1] 38,40,30,589	96,00,764
XII. Málwah	24,06,95,052	60,17,376
New *Ṣúbahs*		
XIII. Berár [2] (from the *taḳsim jam'a*)	69,50,44,682	1,73,76,117
XIV. Khandés [3]	30,25,29,488	75,63,237
XV. Ahmadnagar (not entered).		
Tatah	6,62,51,393	16,56,284
		14,19,09,576[4]
Grand total	5,67,63,83,383 *dáms*, at the rate of 40 *dáms* per rupee = Rs. 14,19,09,584.	

are framed, viz., 18 *dínárs* = 1 *tumán*, each local *tumán* being = 800 *dáms*. A *note* is attached to the effect that the *tumán* of Khorásán is 30 rupees, and that of Irák 40 rupees.

[1] The Multán return, in the preliminary statement, is 15,14,03,619, both in the Calcutta revised text and in Gladwin's old translation. The above figures exhibit the combined *taḳsim jam'a* or detail apportionment of the revenue of the several districts included in the Ṣúbah, entered in the working or administrative lists.

[2] This return is taken from the detailed statements, pp. 61–68. The returns are clearly imperfect, and filled up with fanciful figures in the lower totals, a fact which contrasts in a marked manner with the precision observed in the minor figures of the revenues of the more definitely settled provinces. The total here obtained, however, does not differ very materially from the summary of local *tankahs* quoted below from another part of the work, though it seems to indicate a later manipulation and elaboration of accounts. "This *ṣúbah* (Berár) contains 13 *sirkárs* divided into 142 *pergunnahs*. The *tankah* of this country is equal to eight of those of Dehli. Originally the amount of revenue was 3½ *krors* of *tankahs*, or 56 *krors* of *dáms;* . . . during the government of Sultán Murád the amount rose to 64,26,03,272 *dáms*."—Áín-i Akbari, Gladwin, ii. p. 74.

[3] The introductory summary of the Ṣúbah of Khandés (p. 66) estimates the revenue at 12,64,762 Berári *tankahs*, at 24 *dáms* the *tankah*, that is to say, at 3,03,54,288 *dáms;* but the distribution list at p. 60, second part, raises the sum total to 1,26,47,062 *tankahs*, or 30,25,29,488 *dáms*. There is clearly an error of figures in the first quotation, which the detailed totals of the 32 *pergunnahs* in themselves suffice to prove, as they mount up in simple addition to the still larger sum of 1,55,46,863 *tankahs*.

[4] There is a slight reduction in this total of 8 rupees, consequent upon the loss of the small fractions of *dáms*, which have been left out of the calculation.

I obtain a curious confirmation of the approximate correctness of these revised figures in a return that has been preserved, fortuitously, amid the more ample specifications of the revenues of Aurangzéb, in a Persian MS. now in the East India Library (No. 1387), which is stated to have been copied in A.H. 1195 (A.D. 1780–1), from documents in the possession of the "Nawáb Vizír," *for* "Mr. Richard Johnson." The work professes to be the "Dastúr al 'Amal of Rája Todar Mall,"[1] but the transcriber's note at the conclusion points merely to the application of his revenue system under Sháh Jahán, Rája Rughonáth dás. The opening passage of this compilation contains two entries of the grand totals of the revenues of Hindústán, the one referring to the enhanced revenues for 21 Ṣúbahs, entered in full in the body of the work, and amounting to 13,80,23,56,030 *dáms*, the other under the heading of صوبجات هندوستان بهشت نشان with its "13 Ṣúbahs and 91 Sirkárs," confines itself to the modest sum of 6,63,29,76,338 *dáms* (Rs. 16,58,24,408= £16,582,440), which probably truly represents an authorized increase in Akbar's income upon the earlier 6,62,97,55,246 *dáms*, already deduced from the amended text of the Ā'ín-i Akbari.

In attempting to fix the fiscal returns of the land at any given epoch, it must, primarily, be recognized that India is, and ever has been a relatively poor country, depending mainly upon the produce of its soil and the industries of its prolific people. The revenues of India then, as now, followed the

[1] *Dastúr al 'Amals* are difficult to describe, as it is rash to say what they may not contain amid the multifarious instructions to Revenue Officers. They combine occasionally a court guide, a civil list, an army list, a diary of the period, summaries of revenue returns, home and foreign; practical hints about measures, weights, and coins; with itineraries, and all manner of useful and instructive information.

type of her own great ant-hills, and were built up of innumerable minute accessions and aggregations. Going back to earlier periods, we find that the whole theory of the Hindú law of taxation proceeded upon the primitive village system—that the elected authority, or *Rája*, should take his portion of all gains, of whatever description local knowledge could reduce into a tangible form. In such a state of society the produce of the land was obvious to the sight, and required but slight check or definition, more especially as it formed but a small proportion of the annual assets of a *quasi*-pastoral township. Hence we find the ruler claiming all manner of odd items, extending to his share of commercial profits, one day in the month of the arms and sinews of men, and descending even to a quota of the grass of the fields and the leaves of trees for the State granary.[1]

[1] The Laws of Manu specify the king's taxes in the subjoined terms:—

129. As the leech, the suckling calf, and the bee, take their natural food by little and little, thus must a king draw from his dominions an annual revenue.

130. Of cattle, of gems, of gold and silver, *added each year to the capital stock*, a fiftieth part may be taken by the king; of grain, an eighth part, a sixth, or a twelfth, *according to the difference of the soil and the labour necessary to cultivate it*. [The italics indicate additions by the native commentators.]

131. He may also take a sixth part of the clear annual increase of trees, flesh-meat, honey, clarified butter, perfumes, medical substances, liquids, flowers, roots, and fruit.

132. Of gathered leaves, potherbs, grass, utensils made with leather or cane, earthen pots, and all things made of stone.

In addition to these demands, the king was entitled to graduated taxes on merchandize (127), to be reduced to "a mere trifle" on "petty traffic" (137). And in the case of those "who support themselves by labour," payment of State dues was made in kind, in the form of "a day's work in each month" (138). A source of income seemingly much relied upon was the unclaimed property, more especially that to which there was no heir, which reverted in its entirety to the State (viii. 30); and, lastly, must be reckoned the royalty of half upon "old hoards," treasure trove, and "the precious minerals of the earth" (39). The ferry fees, which are specified in full in other sections of the Law, must also have formed an important item of the royal income.—The Institutes of Manu, C. G. Haughton. London, 1825.

So things went on, seemingly with little essential change, till Akbar made his first move towards fixed returns and money payments; when it is instructive to note that, in accord with the "quarter of wheat," at $3\frac{6}{10}$ pence, and a day's labour at $1\frac{8}{10}$ pence, the revenue assessment of this magnificent empire was made in a coin nearly corresponding with our own halfpenny,[1] a fit and needful concession to the limited means of the cultivators at large, whose small payments or estimates in kind would have been lost or obscured in the ordinary fractions of a rupee; so that, in the length and breadth of the land, no less than 15,360,000,000 pieces of money, or their equivalent value, had to be haggled over before the Mughal's treasury was filled.

Akbar claims to have abolished many of these vexatious taxes, which it is admitted "used to equal the quit-rent of Hindústán."[2] A full enumeration of the cesses in question is given in the table below, and among other State demands thus abandoned figures the especially Muhammadan *Jiziah*, or Poll-tax (see "Chronicles," note 5, p. 272), levied upon unbelievers. This, in effect, constituted a rough species of Income-tax, being graduated according to the means of the different classes of the Hindú community. It may be said to have been invidious, in the one sense; but it was simple, easily collected, and had none of the odious inquisitorial adjuncts of the British Income-tax. The great objection,

[1] The £32,000,000 noticed by Nizám-ud-dín Ahmad at p. 7 multiplied by 480, or the number of halfpence in the £ sterling. The *dám* was in effect 2·4 farthings (see p. 430) if calculated at the ordinary rate of 2*s*. per rupee; but, at 2*s*. 6*d*. per rupee, the *dám* would be equivalent to three farthings.

[2] Gladwin, i. p. 359. The original passage runs—وبیشتر وجوهات که برابر محصول هندوستان بود بایزد شکرانه بخشایش یافت —Calcutta text, p. 301.

however, to the *Jiziah* was the irregularity with which it was enforced, according to the momentary temper or religious phase of thought of the ruler for the time being. It had been pushed to an extreme, in an excess of zeal, by Fírúz Sháh, who was otherwise so fully *en rapport* with the wants and ideas of his people; and after varying fortunes under succeeding princes, it was denounced by Akbar in his anti-Muhammadan infatuation; while Aurangzéb again revived it, in full, in the most persecuting spirit of Islám.

List of Taxes Remitted or Reduced by Akbar.[1]

1. جزيه *Jiziah*, Poll-tax.
Class A, at 40 rupees; B, 20 rupees; C, 10 rupees. [This is Fírúz Sháh's rate, "Chronicles," p. 435. There is no positive return in the Áín-i Akbari.]

2. ميربحري *Mírbahri*, Port-dues and Ferry-fees.
[Sea Customs reduced to 2½ per cent., Tonnage dues on River navigation fixed at "1 rupee per *kos* per 1000 *mans*," (or, roughly, 2 shillings per 2¼ miles for every 24·5 tons.) Tax on Ferries graduated at from 10 *dáms* for an elephant to $\frac{1}{16}$ of a *dám* for the lowest beast of burthen.]

3. كر *Kar* [S. कर], Tax upon pilgrims and religious assemblages.
[An avowedly expansive demand, at the option of the ruling power.]

4. گاو شماري *Gáu shumári*, Tax on cattle.

5. سر درختي *Sar darakhti*, Tax on trees.

6. پيشكش *Peshkash*, Thank-offerings on appointments.

7. فروق و اقسام پيشه *Farúk wa Aksám-i-peshah*, Trade licences.

8. داروغگانه *Dároghgánah*, Fees to Dárógháa.

9. تحصيلداري *Tahsíldári*, Fees to Tehsíldárs.

10. فوطه داري *Fotah dári*, Fees to Treasurers.

[1] Áín-i Akbari, Calcutta Persian Text, p. 301; Gladwin's Translation, i. p. 359.

11. سلامي *Salámi*, Fees to Landlords.

[Like many other local terms, liable to cover very irregular exactions.]

12. وجه كرايه *Wajh kiráyah*, Fees on hiring or letting.

13. خريطه *Kharítah*, Fees for bags on cash payments.

14. صرافي *Ṣarráfi*, Fees on verification of coins.

حاصل بازار *Háṣil-i-bázár*, MARKET DUES on the sale of—

15. نخّاس *Nakhkhás*, Cattle.

16. سن *San*, Hemp.

17. كنبل *Kambal*, Blankets.

18. روغن *Róghan*, Ghí (clarified butter).

19. ادهوڑي *Adhúṛi*, Hides.

20. كيّالي *Kaiyáli*, Rough estimate measurements [or appraisements, *in opposition to*]

21. وزاني *Wazáni*, *Absolute* weighments.

22. قصّابي *Kaṣṣábi*, Slaughtering (animals).

23. دبّاغي *Dabbághi*, Tanning.

24. قماربازي *Kimár bázi*, Gambling (with dice).

25. قنلغه ساوري [كتلا سازي] Sawing planks, Timber-yards.

26. راهداري *Ráh dári*, Transit duties.

27. پگ *Pag*,[1] "A turband."

[Fees on investiture, installation, etc.]

28. دودي *Dúdi*, "Smoke," hearth tax.

29. رسم خانه *Rasm khánah*, Sale of houses.

[Payable both by buyer and seller.]

30. نمكي *Nimaki*, Manufacture of salt.

[1] One of the *Chaubáchha* or four *báchhs* (assessments) of the Dehli territory. 1. *Pág*. 2. *Tág*, "the cloth worn round a child's waist." 3. *Kúḍi* or *Korí*, "a hearth." 4. *Púnchhi*, "a tail," "cattle."—Wilson's Glossary. Elliot's Glossary, i. p. 46, notices other minor cesses under *Palkaṭi*, i.e. *Pala* or *Jharberi*, "cuttings;" *Daranti*, "a sickle;" *Khurpa*, "a grass trowel," or primitive hand-spud.

31. بلكتي *Balkaṭi*, Tax exacted on the commencement of the harvest. [*Bál káṭi*, "cutting ears of corn."]

32. پتي نمد *Pati namad*, Coarse felts (Numdás).

33. چونه كري *Chúnah kari*, Manufacture of lime.

34. خماري *Khammári*, Sale of intoxicating liquors.

35. دلالي *Dalálí*, Brokerage.

36. ماهي گيري *Máhi Gíri*, Fishing.

37. حاصل درخت آل *Haṣil drakht-i-ál*, Dye (*Morinda citrifolia*).

38. سائر جهات, and various other charges and demands known under the general denomination of *Sáyr Jihát*.

The final return of Akbar's series is derived from the publication of De Laët,[1] under information supplied to him by P. Vanden Broecke, President of the Dutch Factory at Surat, who was intimately conversant with the commerce and exchanges of the day, and must have had access to good copies of the Áín-i Akbari, or other official papers, to have enabled him to supply the deficiencies in our extant versions. Singular to say, the data here contributed completely establish the correctness of my proposed rectification of our modern MSS., and subsidiarily of Gladwin's Translation, in

[1] De Imperio Magni Mogolis, sive India Vera, Joannes de Laët. Lugduni Batavorum, ex officina Elzeviriana, 1631. The section of the work from which the extract, now reprinted, is taken, constitutes the tenth or supplementary chapter on Indian history, derived from contemporary national and other testimony, and translated into Latin from the Dutch. The dates of events are carried down to A.D. 1628.

My attention was first attracted to this curious and very rare work by an excellent article in the *Calcutta Review* (October, 1870, January, 1871), on the "Topography of the Mogul Empire," by Mr. E. Lethbridge, which traces, with equal patience and ability, the geographical details furnished by the opening chapter, entitled "Indiæ sive Imperii Magni Mogolis Topographica Descriptio."

the substitution of *six* in place of the "three" in the *arbs*, or "thousand millions," an emendation of the Persian text, I must confess to have been diffident about for the moment,[1] considering the violence it did to all received notions. The extract is otherwise of obvious importance in supporting my determination of the value of the Sikandari Tankah, and, on the other hand, by its full definition of the exchange rate of the *dám* of account, in proving that I was in error in supposing that these pieces were ever reckoned in the revenue returns as the double *dáms* of Ferishtah, etc.[2]

"Coronatione Regis Zianhaengier ubique pervulgata, Legati è Persia, Tartaria, Golconda, Visiapor, Decan, atque à vicinis Radziis, cum opulentissmis donis advenerunt, ut ipsi felicia omnia comprecarentur. Parebant tum ipsi hæ provinciæ *Kandahaer, Kabul, Cassamier, Ghassenie, & Benazaed, Guzaratta, Sinde,* sive *Tatta, Gandhees, Brampor, Barar, Bengala, Orixa, Ode, Malouvv, Agra, Delly,* cum suis limitibus; è quibus annuus census colligitur, uti constat è rationali Regis Achabar; VI Areb & XCVIII Caror, Dam, id est, si ad tangas exigas III Areb & XLIX Caror tangarum; sive secundum monetam regni, XX tangas in singulas rupias computando; aut I Caror tangarum in V lack rupiar. XVII Caror. & XLV

[1] "Chronicles," p. 388, *note* 3.

[2] pp. 369, 387. The demi-official *Dastúr al 'Amals* of the third year of Aurangzéb, to which further reference will be made in the body of the text, specify in detail the several rates of exchange prevailing at this later period, and discriminate the $\frac{1}{40}$ rupee *dám* by the term *tankhwáhi*, or "revenue" *dám*. As the passage in question is open to comment, I annex the original Persian.

یکروپیه‌را شانزده آنه مقرر است و آنه‌را بیست دام مقرر و دیگر
دام تنخواهي یک روپیه‌را چهل دام میشود و دام خام یک پل‌را
بیست و پنج دام مقرر است

—Addit. MSS. British Museum, Nos. 6598 and 6599. See also pp. 158, 360.

Lack rupiarum: atque universus hic annuus census in Magnates, Ducesque & stipendia militum effunditur. De Thesauris à Rege Achabare relictis alibi diximus" (pp. 206–7).

JAHÁNGÍR'S REVENUES.

The next division of the subject embraces the reports of our own countrymen trading with India, or other Englishmen who chanced to reach the Court of the Great Mughal.

Prominent among these is Capt. William Hawkins,[1] who, on his arrival at Agrah, in April, 1609, found himself at once in high esteem with the Emperor Jahángír, in virtue of his knowledge of "Turkish." For a time there was no limit to the royal favour.[2] Hawkins was elevated to a place among the nobles of the land under the title of *Inglis Khán* (English Lord); had a stipend assigned to him; and his Majesty went so far, with a view to retain him near his person, as to offer to select for him a "white maiden from his palace," who should become a Christian by imperial command. Hawkins,

[1] I have elsewhere quoted him as "Richard Hawkins." My mistake in the Christian name was due to "Murray's Travels in Asia," (ii. p. 126), where he is so designated.

[2] "According to command, I resorted to the Court, where I had daily conference with the king. Both night and day his delight was very much to talke with me both of the affaires of England and other countries. . . . . Many days and weeks being past, and I now in great favour with the king; . . . . and now continuing these great favours with the king, being continually in his sight, for the one halfe of foure and twentie hours serving him day and night. . . . [When the reverse came], Abd al Hasan, the hostile *vazír*, 'gave order, that I be suffered no more to enter within the red rayles, which is a place of honour, where all my time I was placed very neere to the king, in which place there were but five men in the kingdom before me.'"—Purchas, i. cap. 7, sec. 2, pp. 209–13; Kerr's Voyages, viii. 252.

however, evaded this compliment, and compromised the difficulty by accepting an Armenian wife, "a Christian of honest descent." But the growing jealousy of the more bigoted Muslim officers of the Court, at the consideration shown to the Nazarenes, was brought to a climax by the baptism, at the King's instance, of the three sons of his brother, inconveniently near relations, who, to use the words of William Finch, were "conducted to the church by all the Christians in the city, to the number of about sixty horse, Captain Hawkins being at their head, with St. George's ensign carried before him, in honour of England."[1]

Hawkins left India in 1611, and died on his passage home. His narrative was originally embodied in a report, written by himself, addressed to the "English Company," from which the following extract is taken:—[2]

"The King's yearly income of his Crowne Land is fiftie Crou of Rupias, every Crou is 100 Leckes, and every Leck is an hundred thousand Rupiæ.[3]

"The compasse of his countrey is two yeares travell with carravan, to say, from Candahar to Agra, from Soughtare

[1] "Narrative of William Finch, Merchant, who accompanied Capt. Hawkins." —Purchas, i. 414; Kerr, viii. 287.

[2] Kerr remarks upon Wm. Hawkins's narrative. "Captain Hawkins in the Dragon accompanied Captain Keeling, in the third voyage fitted out by the English Company; and Finch was in the same vessel with Hawkins, and accompanied him into the country of the Mogul. The present narrative is said, in its title in the Pilgrims, to have been written to the Company, and evidently appears to have been penned by Hawkins himself, without any semblance of having been subjected to the rude pruning knife of Purchas."—Kerr's Voyages, viii. p. 220.

[3] The marginal note in Purchas adds, "the rupia is 2 shillings sterling; some say 2*s.* 3*d.*, some 2*s.* 6*d.*" Terry, in 1616, speaks of the rupees as "of divers values, the meanest being worth 2 shillings, and the best about 2*s.* 9*d.*"—Purchas, ii. p. 146; Kerr, ix. p. 292.

"Argentea autem per Rupias . quæ communiter valent duos solidos et Novem denarios Angl. interdum etiam tantum duos."—De Laët, p. 155.

[Satgáon] in Bengala to Agra, from Cabul to Agra, from Decan to Agra, from Surat to Agra, from Tatta in Sinde to Agra. Agra is in a manner the heart of all his kingdomes." —Purchas, i. 216.

This statement of the Revenues of India, in 1609–11, must be admitted to be fully definite in its terms, and encumbered with no hesitating doubts; as to its correctness, or the sufficiency of the deponent's knowledge, there can equally be no reasonable ground of objection.[1] Hawkins was an experienced trader, who, in the course of his dealings, had necessarily to master systems of exchange and money values, and who, later in the day, had exceptional sources of information regarding the taxation and general administration of the country, of which he has rendered a more or less comprehensive account. I should not quote him with confidence upon any question which concerned the geography of those portions of the continent he himself had not seen, but I am quite prepared to rely upon him in matters coming fairly within his own cognizance. The boon companion of the reigning monarch, a stipendiary noble of the land, with whose manners and customs he so readily identified himself,

[1] One correction is, however, clearly necessary in the old English term of the "crowne land," which cannot be taken to mean *land* revenue alone, but must be held to comprehend the Imperial *estate* in its largest sense, including taxes, customs, and all other miscellaneous receipts, of which the author himself gives a casual outline. As an instance of how these incidental items were liable to affect the annual totals, Hawkins makes mention, as within his own knowledge, of the King taking possession of the estate of one of his subjects at his death, when, "besides jewels, silver, and other valuables, his treasure in gold only amounted to 60 *mans*, every *man* being 55 pounds weight." The royal title to succeed to the effects of deceased persons was a constant grievance to our own countrymen, and a bar to its exercise is inserted in most of our early treaties. *E.g.* Thomas Best's Convention, 1612, para. 8 (Kerr, ix. p. 101); Roe's Treaty, para. 11 (Kerr, ix. p. 272).

could have no difficulty in obtaining a correct sum total of the Exchequer balance sheet, when he was admitted to a knowledge so much more likely to have been accorded with reserve of the absolute contents of the royal treasury itself.[1]

But, in truth, the officials of the day seem to have had no reticence in imparting the financial circumstances surrounding State dignities; even Sir T. Roe, who was far less at home, when Europeans had already lost something of their early prestige, was able to obtain a free report upon the special provincial income and expenditure of his friend the Governor of Patna,[2] though, as he was on more distant

[1] W. Hawkins's account of the treasures of Jahángír embraces the following details (Purchas, i. p. 217):—

	Gold.	Rupees.
a.	In primis Seraffines Ecberi—60 *laks*, @ 10 rupees each......... =	6,00,00,000
b.	Of another sorte of coyne of 1000 Rs. each—20,000 pieces...... =	2,00,00,000
c.	„ „ 500 „ 10,000 „ ...... =	50,00,000
d.	Of another sort of gold of 20 *tolahs*—30,000 pieces (6,00,000×10) =	60,00,000
e.	„ „ 10 „ 25,000 „ (2,50,000×10) =	25,00,000
f.	„ „ 5 „ 50,000 „ (2,50,000×10) =	25,00,000
	Silver.	
a.	Akbari rupees.................................. 13 *kror*..................... =	13,00,00,000
b.	"Coyne of Selim Sháh, this king," of 100 *tolahs*, 50,000 pieces =	50,00,000
c.	„ „ „ 50 „ 1,00,000 „ =	50,00,000
d.	„ „ „ 30 „ 40,000 „ =	12,00,000
e.	„ „ „ 20 „ 30,000 „ =	6,00,000
f.	„ „ „ 10 „ 20,000 „ =	2,00,000
g.	„ „ „ 5 „ 25.000 „ =	1,25,000
h.	Of a certain money that is called Savoy (Sauoy), which is a *tole* ¼, of these there are 2,00,000.. =	2,50,000
i.	Of Iagaries, whereof 5 make 6 *toles*, there is 1,00,000. "More should have been coyned of this stampe, but the contrary was commanded" .... =	1,20,000
		Rs. 23,84,95,000
		or £ 23,849,500

[2] Sir Thomas Roe, speaking of Jamál-ud-dín Husain, Subahdár of Patna, says, "He showed me a book containing the annals of all memorable actions of his time,

terms with leading men of the Court, he, perhaps, wisely confined himself, in his notice of the Imperial resources, to the generalities of the subjoined extract: "In revenue he doubtless exceeds either Turk or Persian, or any Eastern Prince, the sums I dare not name." (Letter of Sir T. Roe, Ambassador of James I. at the Court of Agrah, to the Archbishop of Canterbury, dated Ajmír, 1615.)[1]

Thomas Coryate, writing from Ajmír in the same year, and who in other places rather repeats Sir T. Roe,[2] adverts incidentally to the revenues of Jahángír in the following terms: "His dominions are very extensive, being about 4000 English miles in circumference, nearly answerable to the compass of the Turkish territories; or, if the Mogul kingdom be in any way inferior in size to that empire, it is more than equally endowed with a fertile soil beyond that of any other country, and in having its territory connected together in one goodly continent, within which no other prince possesses one single foot of land. The yearly revenue of the Mogul extends to forty millions of crowns, of six shillings each, while that of the Turk does not exceed fifteen millions, as I was credibly

which he daily committed to record, and offered me a copy if I would procure it to be translated. This also treated concerning the king's revenue, and the manner in which it was raised, besides confiscations, gifts, and deductions upon the great men. He showed me that the government of every province paid yearly a certain rent to the king. Thus for his government at Patna, he gave yearly to the king eleven laks of rupees; all other profits of the government being his own, he having entire power and authority to take what he thought fit. His government was estimated at 5000 horse, the pay of each being 200 rupees yearly, of which he only kept 1500 on foot, being allowed the surplus as dead pay. Besides which, he had a daily pension of 1000 rupees, and enjoyed some smaller governments."—Churchill, i. 633; Kerr's Voyages, ix. p. 282.

[1] Churchill's Voyages, i. p. 659.

[2] Purchas, i. p. 594; Kerr, ix. pp. 422, 428.

informed at Constantinople; nor that of the Sophy five millions."

I allow this last extract to stand for what it is worth; it is difficult to reconcile its terms with other items of nearly contemporaneous evidence.[1] The resulting total of £12,000,000 for the Imperial income is clearly far below the mark, even if applied to exclusively *land* revenue; and the system of reckoning by "crowns of six shillings each" is altogether exceptional, and appears in curious contrast to another passage in the same letter, where the writer speaks of the present which reached the Emperor, during his stay at Ajmír, to the "value of ten of their lacks, a lack being £10,000 sterling."

As this was Coryate's first letter after his arrival at Ajmír, when he was confessedly ignorant of Persian, it is scarcely worth while dwelling upon his apparent errors, from which we may charitably exonerate his subsequently declared patron, Sir T. Roe.[2]

[1] Purchas, in a side-note to this letter, adds, "Of his revenues and of all other things of this State, reade Captain Hawkins, his relations, who had better meanes and judgement to know them." Terry speaks of Coryate as "notus nimis omnibus," and praises him highly, but with discrimination. Coryate died near Surat in December, 1617. See Terry's work, separate edition, London, 1727, reprinted from the earlier edition of 1655, pp. 55–73.

[2] By far the most intelligent observer of all our countrymen in India at this period was Edward Terry, the Chaplain to Sir T. Roe. The Oxford M.A., however, laboured under disadvantages in regard to free intercourse with the Court officials, and possibly for this reason tells us nothing about the revenues. His full geographical summary was the earliest contribution to the knowledge of the day, and forms the basis of De Laët's amplified detail. Terry has left on record some notes on the coinage, which are curious. "All the coin or bullion that comes to this country is presently melted down and refined, and coined with the stamp of the Mogul, being his name and titles in Persian characters. This coin is purer silver than any other that I know, being of virgin silver without alloy,

SHÁH JAHÁN'S REVENUES.

Abd ul Hamíd, the author of the Bádsháh Námah,[1] prefaces his account of the revenues of Sháh Jahán by a definition of the extent and boundaries of the empire, which he calculates as "in length, from Láhri Bandar to Sílhet, close upon 2000 *kos Pádsháhi*, each *kos* consisting of 5000 cubits (ذراع), and each cubit of 42 fingers;[2] and in breadth, from the Fort of Bust to the Fort of Ausah (اوسه *Orissa*), about 1500 *kos*," comprising within its limits 22 *Ṣúbahs* and 4,350 subdivisional *Parganas*. . . . The whole yielding a revenue of 880 *krors*, or 8 *arbs* and 80 *krors* of *dáms* (8,80,00,00,000 *dáms*÷40= 22,00,00,000 rupees÷10=£22,000,000).

so that in the Spanish dollar, the purest money in Europe, there is some loss. Their money is called *rupees*. . . . This is their general money of account. . . . That which passes current for small change is brass money, which they call *pices*, of which three, or thereabout, are worth an English penny. These are made so massy, that the brass in them, when put to other uses, is well worth the quantity of silver at which they are rated. Their silver money is made both square and round, but so thick that it never breaks or wears out."—E. Terry (in Kerr, ix. p. 392).

[1] The Bádsháh Námah comprises the history of the reign of Sháh Jahán from his accession in A.H. 1037 (A.D. 1627) to the close of the thirtieth year of his reign. The first and second volumes are by 'Abd ul Hamíd Láhori, who died in A.H. 1065, when the work was continued by Muhammad Wáris. An edition of the text, embracing the two opening volumes, has been published in the Calcutta Bibliotheca Indica.

[2] See "Chronicles," pp. 371–73. The Sikandari *gaz* was 32 fingers, the Akbari 46, and the Iláhi 41 fingers. The Sháh Jahán Námah has گز in lieu of ذراع.

The revenue returns of the 22 *Ṣúbahs* and the *Viláyat* of Baglánah are given as follows:—

		DÁMS.	RUPEES.
1.	Dehli	1,00,00,00,000	2,50,00,000
2.	Agrah	90,00,00,000	2,25,00,000
3.	Láhor	90,00,00,000	2,25,00,000
4.	Ajmír	60,00,00,000	1,50,00,000
5.	Daulatábád	55,00,00,000	1,37,50,000
6.	Berár	55,00,00,000	1,37,50,000
7.	Ahmadábád	53,00,00,000	1,32,50,000
8.	Bengal	50,00,00,000	1,25,00,000
9.	Allahábád	40,00,00,000	1,00,00,000
10.	Bihár	40,00,00,000	1,00,00,000
11.	Málwah	40,00,00,000	1,00,00,000
12.	Khandés	40,00,00,000	1,00,00,000
13.	Oude	30,00,00,000	75,00,000
14.	Telingánah	30,00,00,000	75,00,000
15.	Multán	28,00,00,000	70,00,000
16.	Orissa	20,00,00,000	50,00,000
17.	Kábul	16,00,00,000	40,00,000
18.	Kashmír	15,00,00,000	37,50,000
19.	Ṭaṭah	8,00,00,000	20,00,000
20.	Balkh	8,00,00,000	20,00,000
21.	Kandahár	6,00,00,000	15,00,000
22.	Badakhshán	4,00,00,000	10,00,000
23.	Baglánah	2,00,00,000	5,00,000
		8,80,00,00,000	22,00,00,000

Having completed the specification of the revenues of the several divisions, the author observes, that at the accession of Sháh Jahán the State income only amounted to 700 *krors* of *dáms* (Rs. 17,50,00,000), but that during the twenty initial years of the new reign prosperity had made material progress in the land, and the acquisitions in the Dakhan, accounted for in detail, had contributed to the enhanced total entered in the return. After some further remarks upon the change of the designation of the old Ṣúbah of Daulatábád to that of Ahmadnagar, the writer somewhat abruptly introduces a third return, which may be supposed to refer to the Hijrah years 1057–8 (A.D. 1647–8), as the latter date occurs in a subsequent page, though the author himself did not die till A.H. 1065 (A.D. 1654–5), and may have gone on adding to and improving his work continuously up to the end of his life.

The supplementary passage quoted below[1] is to the effect

[1] از همگي ولايات سابق و لاحق صد و بيست كرور* دام خالصه مقرري است كه موافق دوازده ماه سه كرور* روپيه حاصل آنست محصول باقي برين قياس بايد نمود - پيشتر اين قدر خالصه نبود درين عهد ابدپيوند از وسعت مملكت قرار يافته

—Calcutta *printed* Persian text, vol. ii. p. 712.

As I had some doubts about the authenticity of this possibly interpolated passage, I consulted a MS. Pádsháh Námah in the British Museum (Addit. No. 26,222), which was found to correspond with the above version. And M. Sachau was so obliging as to examine for me the single MS. copy of the second volume of the work in the Bodleian Library (MS. Elliot, No. 368, engrossed in A.H. 1109, A.D. 1697), which varies only to the extent of unaccountably omitting the words placed between the *stars* in the above text.

The nearly contemporary Sháh Jahán Námah of *K*ashná Ináyat Khán slightly modifies the tenor of the sentence, without altering the relative amounts.

از جمله اين صد و بيست كرور دام خالصه مقرري است كه موافق دوازده ماهي سه كرور روپيه حاصل دارد

—Addit. MS. British Museum, شاه جهان نامه No. 20,735, p. 304. "The King of Dehli's own copy, 1815."

Mr. Morley, in his Catalogue of the Royal Asiatic Society's MSS., remarks that, calculating the income from the old and newly annexed provinces, the monthly revenue of the empire may be taken as "120,00,00,000 *dáms*, or 3,00,00,000 rupees," giving an annual return of 36,00,00,000 rupees or £36,000,000, at the lowest estimate of exchange.[1] It is, of course, possible that the intention in the citation of this lump sum may have been to cover revenue from all sources; but the context certainly does not necessitate such a conclusion,[2] though it

that "this work is little more than an abridgment of the Bádsháh Námah of 'Abd ul Hamíd." The author, however, occupied a good position at Court, and was quite competent to correct or improve any shortcomings in the original, upon which he based his history. He died in A.H. 1077 (A.D. 1666).

Kháfi Khán, who quotes what he calls the Sháh Jahán Námah (the name is used indifferently, without much discrimination, for the Bádsháh Námah), does not reproduce this passage, but heads the detail list above given with the words

جمع دامي بيست و يک صوبهٔ هندوستان لغايت سنه بيست جلوس صاحب قران که بازکم و زياده شده باشد بدين تفصيل

—Calcutta Text, p. 672.

Kháfi Khán's work is otherwise entitled the "Muntakhab-i-Lubb-i-Lubáb." It was composed in Aurangzéb's reign, but only published in A.H. 1145 (A.D. 1732).

[1] The word خالصه, *Khálṣah*, implies conventionally *State land*, or, rather, in general terms, the revenue of land coming directly into the State coffers, as distinguished from the same rents or dues when temporarily assigned or permanently alienated for other objects, in diminution of the normal governmental demand. Khálṣah, however, is a term whose application was generally misunderstood by early European travellers, and hence we find them saying "all the land is his," *i.e.* the King's; but, in truth, his title merely extended to the share of the State, noticed at pp. 8, 15. The King could, of course, alienate his *own* or "the *Khálṣah*" demand, plus the cost of collection, and the inevitable rights, titles, and perquisites incident to local government, but all these concessions could be resumed again by a stroke of the pen. These grants may have been called by many names, but "during pleasure" was the inexorable rule. In its home sense, the purport of the word Khálṣah was frequently modified, so that in the Punjáb it came at last to indicate the State itself.

[2] It must be borne in mind that wherever these estimates are made on the basis of the rate of 40 *dáms* to the rupee, this of itself implies the corresponding

will, perhaps, be as well to limit the interpretation of the passage to an assertion that the monarch had available for ordinary expenses an average of 3,00,00,000 rupees per month, after deducting all assignments, alienations, etc. A construction in this sense is the more imperative, seeing that the author is specially given to "averages," every one of his minor items of the revenue tables being avowedly reduced to a mean sum in even figures. We thus obtain three several returns—(1) for the year of Jahángír's death, A.H. 1037, or A.D. 1627–8, amounting to £17,500,000; (2) for A.D. 1648–9, £22,000,000; and (3) for A.D. 1647–8, or some later period, a general or mixed total of £36,000,000.

Having exhausted the semi-official Chronicles of the Court scribes, and the casual contributions of the English pioneers in the camps of the Great Mughal, we have now to test the evidence of Europeans of other nationalities who had opportunities, more or less complete, of obtaining information regarding the finances of India during the reigns of Sháh Jahán and Aurangzéb.

First in order among these, figures the name of J. A. de Mandelsloe, who refers only incidentally to the revenues of the Mughal Empire in A.D. 1638, in the following terms, as rendered into English:—"According to the roll of the kingdom, the provinces of Kandahár, Dehli, Bengal, Orixa, and some others, bring in a yearly revenue of 87,250,000 crowns." (Harris's Collection, i. 762.)

This passage is scarcely definite enough to command any very close examination; but if we might assume that

obligation of recognizing the full value of the best silver coin in circulation (see "Chronicles," p. 421), so that in calculating relative values in English money, even the 2*s.* 6*d.* rate of exchange would bring this total of 36,00,00,000 rupees up to £45,000,000.

Mandelsloe's estimate by "crowns"[1] was intended to represent that number of rupees, as the context seems to imply, and further correct the given sum by the addition of an 0, we should have to admit that the country had already arrived at an approach to the pitch of prosperity claimed for it with more distinctness by later authors in A.D. 1695–7.

An incidental notice of the Revenues of India under Sháh Jahán is to be found in Ramusio, where, in introduction to the detail of the provincial returns of Aurangzéb's income in A.D. 1707 (quoted at large at p. 49 *infrà*), it is stated that "in his father's time the empire consisted of twenty-three provinces, the revenues of which amounted to £27,500,000 of our money; but in the latter end of his father's time the three provinces of Balkh, Kandahár, and Badakhshán were lost, which produced a revenue of £600,000." (Harris, i. 651.) It will be seen, when we come to analyze the full details of the return of Aurangzéb's revenue in A.D. 1707, as reported by this authority, that the total of £27,500,000 here given is obtained by estimating the rupee at 2*s*. 6*d*., which brings us back to the frequently recurring sum assigned to this period of 22,00,00,000 rupees, or, at the lower rate of 2*s*. per rupee, to £22,000,000.

[1] He estimates the value of Akbar's treasure in "crowns and pence," and defines the "crown" as equal to 60 *payses*, which seems to prove that his term "crowns" merely applied to current rupees, an inference which is further established by the total he gives of the treasure itself, as his *cash* return of 19,91,73,333 evidently refers to the same sum as that quoted by De Laët as 19,83,46,666 rupees.—Harris, i. p. 762.

AURANGZÉB'S REVENUES.

Next in progression of dates, we are able to produce more formal official documents regarding the state of the Imperial revenue at and about this period. These consist of the assessment tables inserted in the *Dastúr al 'Amals,* or revenue manuals, already referred to, which, in this instance, profess to refer to a *specific* year of the reign of Aurangzéb. As far as can be ascertained, the two MSS. in the British Museum (Addit. Nos. 6598 and 6599) are official and nearly duplicate copies of what purports to be the *Dastúr al 'Amal* of the third year of Aurangzéb, which is further formulated as A.H. 1065 (or A.D. 1654–5).[1] These documents are modern transcripts,[2] but the one was adopted and seemingly recopied for the use of our own fiscal *employés,* as they both bear the oblong seal of the Díwáni of Bengal and Bihár, coupled with the name

[1] The MS. opens as follows:—

دستور العمل معملي حسب الحكم حضور اقدس اعلي حضرت
اورنگزيب عالمگير بادشاه غازي در سنه ٣ جلوس و يكهزار شصت
وپنج هجري از هر صيغه انتخاب نموده * *

[2] MS. No. 6598 has an entry at the end of one of its sections of "Dehli, 28th *Shawdl, San* 28 of Shâh 'Alam," *i.e.* 1789. There is a second revenue return, copied by a different penman, in a later portion of this MS. (p. 130), giving a grand total of "6,63,29,46,338 *dáms* for the 23 Ṣúbahs," seemingly another version of the old settlement of the Áín-i Akbari, which has already been quoted from an independent MS. ("Chronicles," p. 444) in confirmation of my correction of Abul Fazl's figures. The minor items of this illustrative table are intermediate between Abd ul Hamíd's returns and those now given for the third year of Aurangzéb's reign; and the six Ṣúbahs of the Dakhan are separately placed at 6,00,22,22,140 *dáms.*

of "James Grant," and dated in the Bengáli Faṣl, 1193 (A.D. 1786).[1] Among other miscellaneous contents, these MSS. have preserved parallel copies of the revenue returns of Aurangzéb for "20 Ṣúbahs and 2 kingdoms," the amount realizable from which they concur in fixing at 9,62,24,45,846 *dáms* (or Rs. 24,05,61,146=£24,056,114). The aggregate totals for the several provinces, entered in detail in the body of the work, exceed this amount by no less than £2,687,856; and, to the uninitiated, would suggest a doubt as to the correctness of the two returns; whereas, this difference is, in effect, the best test of the relative totals themselves, and conclusive confirmation of the accuracy of the higher figures of the associate sums. The one amount, in short, represents the *gross* returns realized in the provinces, the other the *nett* payments to the Imperial treasury; the difference being the *ten* per cent. allowed to the *'A'mil* or *Kṛoṛi* for collection.[2]

[1] The full legend on the seal is as follows:—

بدارالمهامّ سپه‌سالار انگریز کمپني ديوان صوبه‌جات بنگاله و بهار
وغیره صدر سرشته‌دار و ملاحظه‌فاتر ازصارف جمس کرانت سنه
۱۱۹۳ بنگله

James Grant was one of those admirable Executive officers of our early service in the East who so conscientiously investigated the details of the fiscal administration of our predecessors,—the value of whose work the Government of the day were utterly incapable of appreciating. Mr. Grant's exhaustive returns are to be found in the Fifth Report on Indian Affairs, presented to the House of Commons (1812).

[2] Akbar's *Kṛoṛi*, or collector of a *kṛoṛ* of *dáms*, received eight per cent. on the amount of his realizations, together with other perquisites. In A.D. 1639, under Sháh Jahán, the *Kṛoṛi* or *'A'mil* was invested with the additional duties of *Faujdár*, with an allowance of ten per cent. on the collections. These per-centages were subsequently modified in their details; under S'adullah Khán, five per cent. only was allowed to the *Kṛoṛi*, and of this one per cent. was subsequently deducted. This arrangement was upheld in Aurangzéb's reign, and lasted till the dissolution of the empire.—Elliot's Glossary, i. p. 198.

AURANGZÉB'S REVENUE IN A.D. 1654–5.

		DÁMS.	RUPEES.
1.	Dehli	1,55,88,39,127	3,89,70,978
2.	Agrah	1,36,46,02,117	3,41,15,052
3.	Láhor	1,08,97,59,776	2,72,43,994
4.	Ajmír	64,87,61,685	1,62,19,042
5.	Daulatábád... ...	50,71,60,000	1,26,79,000
6.	Berár	59,06,00,000	1,47,65,000
7.	Ahmadábád ...	86,92,88,069	2,17,32,201
8.	Bengal	45,78,58,000	1,14,46,450
9.	Allahábád	52,78,81,196	1,31,97,029
10.	Bihár	54,53,00,935	1,36,32,523
11.	Malwáh	55,73,17,320	1,39,32,933
12.	Khándés	49,69,30,000	1,24,23,250
13.	Oude	36,39,82,859	90,99,571
14.	Telingana	19,46,08,000	48,65,200
15.	Multán	33,84,21,178	84,60,529
16.	Orissa	22,55,80,000	56,39,500
17.	Kábul	9,70,78,000	24,26,950
18.	Kashmír	11,43,90,000	28,59,750
19.	Ṭaṭah	8,92,30,000	22,30,750
20.	Kandahár	6,00,00,000	15,00,000
	Dáms...	10,69,75,88,262	
	÷40=	26,74,39,706	Rs. 26,74,39,702

Gross return, £26,743,970. Nett return, £24,056,114.

A witness, for whom the greatest reliance might have been claimed, had he expressed more confidence in his own returns, is the celebrated traveller Bernier, who, in his leading narrative, so far neglected the subject of the income of the State as to omit all reference to it in his first edition, only inserting the subjoined table as an appendix to the re-issue of his work. For obvious reasons, he is apologetic regarding the table itself, and expresses his distrust of the grand total, which he clearly considered to be far too large in amount. I confess that I estimate the document at a higher standard than the author was disposed to concede to it; and so far from any excess in the grand total, I am disposed to impute a deficiency, especially in the complete omission of any return for the province of Bengal, and the manifest absence of a nought in the sum assigned for Kashmír.

Bernier tells us nothing of the source from whence he derived his data, nor the precise year to which they refer,[1] but they bear the stamp of a certain degree of authenticity, and, allowing for deficiencies, they fairly fit in with the prior and subsequent returns.

I have allowed them to stand in the form supplied by the French text, but the suggested emendations would raise the sum total by 31,50,000 rupees for the difference in the Kashmíri figures, and some 2,00,00,000 to 2,50,00,000 at the lowest estimate for the revenues of Bengal,[2] which last item Bernier himself, perhaps intentionally, omitted, as he adverts to the temporary antagonism and independence of the province under Sultán Shujah.

[1] His description of Dehli and Agrah was written at Dehli in July, 1663. Subsequent portions of the work were written at Kashmír in the same year. In 1667 Bernier was in Golconda (p. 131); and his letter from Shíráz, on his homeward journey, is dated 1667 (p. 173).

[2] Curious to say, Bernier, among his other errors, has omitted, in his final summary, the *twenty* in the 22 *krors* of rupees, and made the grand total "deux" *krors* only. In this he has been followed mechanically by the Editor of the English translation (London, 1672), who also sums up his total as "above two kourours" of rupees (iv. p. 178). And the mistake has remained undetected in Pinkerton's Collection, viii. p. 234.

"Memoire oublié à inserer dans mon premier Ouvrage pour perfectionner la Carte de l'Indoustan, et savoir les Revenus du Grand Mogol." [1]

		RUPEES.
1.	Dehli...	1,95,25,000
2.	Agrah	2,52,25,000
3.	Láhor	2,46,95,000
4.	Hasmir [2]	2,19,70,000
5.	Gujarát (Ahmadábád) ...	1,33,95,000
6.	Kandahár [3]	19,92,500
7.	Málwah	91,62,500
8.	Patna or Bihár	95,80,000
9.	Allahábád...	94,70,000
10.	Oude [4]	68,30,000
11.	Multán	1,18,40,500
12.	"Jagannat"	72,70,000
13.	Kashmír	3,50,000
14.	Kábul	32,72,500
15.	Tata	23,20,000
16.	Aurangábád	1,72,27,500
17.	"Varada" (Berár)	1,58,75,000
18.	Khándés	1,85,50,000
19.	Telingána [5]	68,85,000
20.	Baglana [6]	5,00,000

Rs. 22,59,35,500 or £22,593,550

[1] Bernier's Voyages, Amsterdam, 1724, vol. ii., p. 354. See also English edition, iv. p. 175.

[2] Qui appartient à un Raja, donne au roi de tribut, etc.

[3] Chiefly under Persia; Perganahs remaining to India pay as above.

[4] Pinkerton's Voyages, viii. p. 61, and English translation, gives Oude as 64,30,000.

[5] "Talengand, qui confine au Royaume de Golkonda du côté de Massipatan, a quarante-trois Pragnas."

[6] "Bagnala qui confine aux terres des Portugais et aux montagnes de Sevagi,

"Suivant ce Memoire que je ne crois pas trop exact ni veritable, le Grand Mogol a de rente tous les ans de ses seules Terres plus de deux Kouroures de Roupies."

The subjoined account of Dr. Gemelli Careri,[1] relating to the year 1695 A.D., is highly interesting in the close approach of the sum named as the *grand total* of the revenues of Aurangzéb (£80,000,000) to that given from the independent testimony of Manucci:—"Of the revenues and wealth of the Great Mogul, an infinite quantity of roupies is continually flowing into the Great Mogul's exchequer; for besides the usual taxes and excessive imposts, the subjects must pay for their land, which is all his. . . . . . I was told that the *Mogul* receives from only his hereditary countries 80 *carores* of *roupies* a year (every *carore* is ten millions); they could give me no certain account of what the conquered kingdoms yield. There is an author, not well acquainted with this affair, who reduces this monarch's revenue to 33 millions (Thevenot, Voy. des. Ind. c. 3, p. 12).[2] Another, on the other side, makes it infinite,

ce Raja qui a saccagé Sourate, a deux Serkars, huit Pragnas." The nidus of the future power of the Mahrattas, "*Bhagelana*," "between the 20th and 21st degree N. latitude."—Hamilton, Rennell, etc.

[1] Gemelli Careri (Jean François), célèbre voyageur italien, né à Naples, vers 1651, mort vers 1725. "Giro del Mondo," Naples, 1699–1700, 6 vol. in 12. In French, Voyage autour du monde, Paris, 1719, new edit. 1776.

[2] The subjoined is Thevenot's return for A.D. 1666:—

		French Livres.
1.	Dehli	37,000,000 to 38,000,000
2.	Agrah...	37,000,000
3.	Láhor...	37,000,000
4.	Ajmír	32,000,000 to 33,000,000
5.	Daulátábad (Aurangábád)..	25,000,000
6.	Berár (Becar)	14,000,000
7.	Ahmadábád	20,500,000
8.	Bengal (including 16) ...	10,000,000 or 9,000,000

and that alone which he says is in the treasury seems fabulous (De Imp. Mog. sive India vera, p. 142).[1] But they that will judge of it by his expenses, must consider that the *Mogul* has dispersed throughout his empire 300,000 horse and 400,000 foot, who have all great pay." (A Voyage Round the World, by Dr. J. F. Gemelli Careri, Churchill's Collection, iv. p. 235.)

As the return of Aurangzéb's revenues contributed by Manucci exhibits the highest amount of taxation realized under the Mughals, it is satisfactory to be able to preface its details by documents, indicating approximate advances in the State income, derived from independent native sources.

The data for the subjoined tables are extracted from the

		French Livres.		French Livres.
9.	Allahábád	14,000,000		
10.	Bihár (Varad)	27,000,000		
11.	Málwah	14,000,000		
12.	Khandes	27,000,000		
13.	Oude	10,000,000		
14.	Telingana	10,000,000		
15.	Multán	17,500,000		
16.	Orissa (Bengal)			
17.	Kábul	4,000,000	to	5,000,000
18.	Kashmír	500,000	to	600,000
19.	Ṭaṭṭa (Sind)	3,400,000		
20.	Balkh			
21.	Kandahár	14,000,000	to	15,000,000
22.	Badakshan			
23.	Baglana*	750,000		
	Total for 20 Provinces	354,650,000	+ 3,100,000 =	357,750,000

* Capital, "Mouler," p. 82.

[1] I can scarcely concur in this criticism. Taking De Laët's own figures, Akbar, with a yearly revenue from land alone of £17,450,000, left in his treasury cash to the amount of £19,834,666, or little more than half a year's income, if we include all sources of taxation. See also Hawkins's return, p. 24; Mandelsloe's return, p. 32 *antè;* and Harris's Collection, i. p. 762.

official statistics embodied in the manuals of the collectors of revenue, conventionally known as "Dastúr al 'Amals." From the number of these authoritative guides still extant, I am able to cite no less than *three*, which bear upon some later epoch of Aurangzéb's reign.[1] The returns contributed, imperfect as they are in their details, are definite and distinct in their totals, and clearly refer to one original official compilation. Unfortunately, the copies available are all modern transcripts, and show unmistakable signs of the ignorance and carelessness of the engrossers, and an entire want of method in checking or reconciling the subordinate items with the larger totals. With all these drawbacks, however, they are quite sufficient for the purpose, now in view, of testing the value of Manucci's sources of information. And here I would desire to explain why I prefer to rely upon external testimony rather than upon the formal papers of the servants of the State: these latter usually refer to a given assessment or settlement of the land revenue for a

[1] MS. A is the work alluded to at p. 14 *suprà*. Many passages in the text indicate that Aurangzéb was reigning at the period of its compilation.

MS. B is a copy of a MS., in the Library of the Asiatic Society of Bengal, made for Sir H. Elliot in 1854. It purports to be a history of the Kings of Dehli, but among other matter it contains a very imperfect return of Sháh Jahán's revenues, many of the items of which accord with the figures furnished by Abd ul Hamíd *Láhori*: but the ignorance of the scribe has converted the *dáms* of the original into the same number of rupees, or forty times the true amount. The Aurangzéb return occurs later in the work, and is unaccompanied by any introduction, except the usual heading of "the Ṣúbahs of the occupied kingdom."

MS. C is a fragment, also copied for Sir H. Elliot; but the original from whence it is derived is not specified. It contains full returns for the 21 Ṣúbahs and 205 Sirkárs; the details of the revenue of the latter are given at large, after the plan adopted in the Áín-i Akbari.

The *raḳams*, or abbreviated word-figures, in which all Indian revenue accounts are kept, are badly formed, and at times difficult to discriminate. The author or transcriber has likewise taken little pains to verify the given sums.

term of years, without marking in any distinct way the incidental fluctuations of absolute collections, the loss of territory, or the spread of conquest. If written up at all, they were probably merely altered for the province or locality in which they were in use; whereas, a competent witness at head-quarters would be in a position to obtain exact information of the actual income for the current year, as it was reported, on immediate realization from the various divisions of the empire.

Of the three MSS. from which the annexed tables have been compiled, two only furnish grand totals of the revenue of the empire, and these sums do not accord with the simple addition of the items entered in detail. MS. C places the State income at 13,80,23,56,030 *dáms*, or 34,50,58,900 *rupees;* MS. A fixes the sum at 13,80,26,56,263 *dáms*, or 34,50,66,406 *rupees.* Amid these conflicting testimonies, and specially desiring to avoid undue enhancements, I had at first selected for comparison the MS. C, which possessed the advantage of the entry of the *sarkár,* or subordinate divisional totals, which are wanting in the other MSS. The insertion of these tests would presumably secure greater accuracy in the reckoning up of the larger items. But, on the other hand, the given returns do not balance, and the difference of the relative amounts not only does not allow for any reduction of the gross sum, as against the nett total, but exhibits a positive loss on the former of 31,87,761 rupees.

Under these circumstances I have adopted the compromise of recognizing the *nett* total of C as against the *gross* returns supplied by B, relatively 35,64,14,317 and 34,50,58,900 rupees, the difference, 1,13,55,417 rupees, may be accepted as a vague approach to the reduced four per cent. allowed for collection, noticed at p. 34.

AURANGZÉB'S REVENUE, FROM THREE INDEPENDENT COPIES OF OFFICIAL RETURNS.

	A. DÁMS.	B. DÁMS.	C. DÁMS.	*Dáms* in column C reduced into Rupees.
1. Dehli	1,22,29,50,177	1,21,29,50,137	1,22,29,50,137	3,05,73,753
2. Agrah	1,14,17,00,157	1,14,17,60,157	96,11,67,015	2,40,29,175
3. Láhor	89,81,32,107	89,81,32,107	89,30,39,419	2,23,25,985
4. Ajmír	65,26,45,702	65,23,45,702	60,29,80,270	1,50,74,506
5. Daulatábád (اورنک اباد)	1,18,30,65,000	1,40,28,44,771	1,18,37,35,000	2,95,93,375
6. Berár (فتح پور)	92,65,45,000	1,09,17,25,271	92,65,45,000	2,31,63,625
7. Ahmadábád (Gujarát)	45,47,45,135	45,47,49,135	53,65,25,000	1,34,13,125
8. Bengal	52,46,36,240	52,46,36,240	52,46,36,140	1,31,15,903
9. Allahábád[1]	45,65,43,012	45,65,43,012	42,13,46,927	1,05,33,673
10. Bihár	40,71,81,000	40,71,81,000	29,43,44,536	73,58,613
11. Málwah	40,39,80,658	40,39,80,658	40,83,46,716	1,02,08,667
12. Khándés	42,06,00,000	59,29,32,347	42,00,00,000	1,05,00,000

13. Oude	32,13,17,119	32,13,17,119	27,95,79,619	69,89,490
14. Telingána (Haiderábád)	1,09,28,65,000	1,09,35,28,000	1,00,28,35,000	2,50,70,875
15. Multán	20,43,49,896	21,43,00,000	19,98,02,318	49,95,057
16. Orissa	14,28,11,000	14,23,21,000	17,28,41,000	43,21,025
17. Kábul	10,43,49,896	16,10,39,357	20,21,81,942	50,54,548
18. Kashmír	22,49,11,397	22,99,00,392	27,79,11,397	69,47,784
19. Ṭaṭah	6,88,16,810	6,88,16,810	6,88,01,000	17,20,025
20. Bidar (محمداباد—ظفراباد)	62,05,50,000	53,07,42,342	82,05,50,000	2,05,13,750
21. Bíjápúr	2,25,48,28,140	2,25,48,27,140	2,25,47,27,140	5,63,68,178
Dáms	13,72,27,23,486	14,25,65,72,697	13,67,48,45,576	Rs. 34,18,71,132
Rs.	34,30,68,087	35,64,14,317	34,18,71,139	

[1] I have corrected the obvious clerical error in MS. A, which assigns the sum of 1,14,17,00,157 *dáms* to Allahábád, into the more reasonable total of 45,65,43,012 *dáms*, given in MS. B. The mistake appears to have arisen from the transcriber repeating the proper Agrah return under the heading of Allahábád.

The following table has been compiled from the French text of Catrou's "Histoire générale de l'Empire du Mogol,"[1] an author who, however worthless in his own proper sphere, derives his information on fiscal matters from the higher authority of the Venetian traveller Manucci.[2] I have not thought it necessary to reproduce the original passage which contributes these figures *in extenso;* but I append in full Catrou's reiteration of the various taxes and sources of revenue which contributed in themselves a second sum equal to the full amount of the *land revenue* pure and simple, as a justification for the abrupt estimate inserted under the head of income from all sources in my concluding recapitulation. At the same time I am bound to expose both the strength and weakness of the evidence of Manucci himself. A man who for nearly fifty years was intimately connected with the reigning powers, albeit as a Frank doctor, had unusual opportunities of observing the peculiarities of the general system of government, so to say, from behind the scenes; and as regards his extracts from official documents,—which he truly says were most rigidly engrossed and preserved at the Court of the Mughal,—there need be no contest as to the completeness of the original papers from which he obtained his knowledge. There are symptoms of incorrect transmutations of the lower figures from the Persian *raḳams,*[3] especially in the

[1] Paris, 4to., 1702. Traduite en Italien, 1718. Second edition, 4 vols. duodecimo, 1725.

[2] "Manucci (Nicolas), Voyageur vénetien, mort vers 1710.

"Il passa aux Indes fut attaché comme premier médecin au fils du grand Mogol Aurangzéb, et quitta ce prince vers 1690.

"Retiré probablement en Portugal, il publia l'ouvrage suivant, devenu rarissime: Istoria de Mogol en tres partes de Nicolas Manuchi, Veneziano; de Reinado de Orangzeb, Guerras de Golconda e Visapour com varios successos até a era de 1700. 3 vol."—*Biog. Universelle.* See also Orme's *Fragments,* iv. p. vi.

[3] The *raḳam* (رقم), or system of numeration in use in the Indian revenue

number of the vacant places in the fifth column, or second place of thousands; but, otherwise, there is very little open to objection in his version. The list from which he took his returns was clearly unconventional in form, and unusually strong and independent in Dakhan totals, which are divided into new heads in the one case, and grouped into novel combinations in others, such as might be expected from the record of the Southern State ledgers of Aurangzéb's son, Sultan Mu'azzam, with whose fortunes Manucci was more directly associated. The flaw, if any, in the general detail, might be charged against the extraordinary amount assigned not only to Bengal itself, but to the unprecedented intrusion of the division of Rájmahal; but it would be more than hazardous to assert, with our present knowledge, that these things were not so, or that these amounts were not realized at any given period, however exceptional the momentary realization may have proved.

tables, consists of a series of signs, abridged from the full Arabic word for the given number: a very terror to young students who desire to commit it to memory mechanically, but simple in the extreme when tested by its primitive elements. It proceeds upon the theory of having separate signs for the units, tens, hundreds, and thousands, the higher numbers being written in the upper lines, while the signs for the thousands, etc., are run consecutively at the foot of the sum, as in the subjoined form:—

Arbs 1. Read to the left.
Krors 2.
Laks 3.
units, tens, hundreds, thousands, 4.

The main difficulty in checking the conventional Indian definition of these sums in the lower totals arises from the slovenly practice in use of discarding the true symbols for *thousands*, and expressing those numbers by ordinary *units* and *tens*, so that unless there chance to be a sign for *a hundred* in the general sum, the written number in the lower line may stand for, say, 20,000 or 20. In the better written MSS. the insertion of the signs سـ settles the question in favour of the thousands, but otherwise it is quite optional to which column of our figures the numbers should be referred. A full, almost needlessly full, table of these symbols is engraved in Stewart's Persian Letters, London, 1825.

TABLE OF THE REVENUES OF AURANGZÉB IN A.D. 1697.

1.	Dehli	1,25,50,000	rupees.
2.	Agrah	2,22,03,550	„
3.	Láhor	2,33,05,000	„
4.	Ajmír	2,19,00,002	„
5.	Gujarát	2,33,95,000	„
6.	Málwah	99,06,250	„
7.	Bihár...	1,21,50,000	„
8.	Multán	50,25,000	„
9.	Kábul	32,07,250	„
10.	Tata	60,02,000	„
11.	Bakar	24,00,000	„
12.	Urecha (Orissa)	57,07,500	„
13.	Kashmír	35,05,000	„
14.	Allahábád	77,38,000	„
15.	Dakhan (*a* in General Table) ...	1,62,04,750	„
16.	Berár...	1,58,07,500	„
17.	Kándés	1,11,05,000	„
18.	Baglánah	68,85,000	„
19.	"Nandé" (Nandair) (*b*)	72,00,000	„
20.	Bengal	4,00,00,000	„
21.	Ujain (*c*)	2,00,00,000	„
22.	Rájmahal	1,00,50,000	„
23.	Bíjápúr	5,00,00,000	„
24.	Golconda	5,00,00,000	„
		38,62,46,802	„

The French epitomist justifies Manucci's data, and continues the illustration of his subject from the Italian's own inspiration in the following terms:—"Ce que nous avons dit jusqu'icy, est un préjugé favorable pour rendre croïable ce que nous allons dire. Sans doute on ne sera plus surpris des immenses revenus que le Mogol recuëille de ses Etats. En voici la liste tirée des archives de l'Empire. L'état du produit de ce grand Domaine, que l'Empereur possède lui seul dans toute l'étenduë de sa Souveraineté, étoit, en l'année 1697, tel que nous l'allons représenter.[1] . . . . . . Le tout supputé fait *trois cens quatre-vingt-sept millions de roupies & cent, quatre-vingt-quatorze mille* (38,71,94,000 rupees, or £38,719,400).[2] Ainsi à prendre les roupies des Indes pour trente sols ou environ de nôtre monnoye de France, le Domaine de l'Empereur Mogol lui produit tous les ans, *cinq cens quatre-vingt millions, sept cens quatre-vingt onze mille livres.* Outre ces revenus fixes du Domaine, qu'on tire seulement des fruits de la terre, le casuel de l'Empire est une autre source de richesses pour l'Empereur. 1°. On exige tous les ans un tribut par tête de tous les Indiens idolâtres. Comme la mort, les voyages, & les fuites de ces anciens habitans de l'Indoustan, en rendent le nombre incertain, on le diminuë beaucoup à l'Empereur. Les gouverneurs profitent de leur déguisement. 2°. Toutes les marchandises, que les Négocians Idolâtres font transporter, payent aux Doüannes cinq pour cent de leur valeur. Oramgzeb a exempté les Mahométans de ces sortes d'impots. 3°. Le blanchissage de cette multitude infinie de toiles qu'on travaille aux Indes, est encore la matière d'un tribut. 4°. La mine de diamans paye à l'Empereur une grosse somme. Il exige pour lui les plus beaux & les plus parfaits; c'est-à-

[1] Selon la manière de compter dans l'Indoustan, un *carol* vaut cent *laqs*, c'est-à-dire, dix millions; & qu'un *laq* vaut cent mille *roupies*: Enfin que les *roupies* valent à peu près *trente sols*, monnoye de France.

[2] My total in the table varies slightly from this amount. There may have been some omissions among the minor items in the French text, while the grand total possibly reproduces the figures of Manucci's original Italian text. Oude, for instance, is not entered at all in the detailed list in Catrou's version.

dire tous ceux qui sont au-dessus de *trois huit*. 5°. Les ports de mer, & particulièrement ceux de Sindi, de Barocha, de Suratte, & de Cambaye, sont taxez à de grosses sommes. Suratte seul rend ordinairement *trente laqs* pour les droits d'entrées, & *onze laqs* pour le profit des monnoyes qu'on y fait battre. 6°. Toute la côte de Coromandel, et les Ports situez sur les bords du Gange, produisent de gros revenus au Souverain. 7°. Ce qui les augmente infiniment c'est l'hêritage qu'il perçoit universellement de tous ses Sujets Mahométans qui sont à sa solde; tous les meubles, tout l'argent, & tous les effets de celui qui meurt, appartiennent de droit à l'Empereur. Par là les femmes des Gouverneurs de Provinces & des Généraux d'armées, sont souvent réduites à une pension modique, & leurs enfans, s'ils sont sans mérite, sont réduits à la mendicité. 8°. Les tributs des Rajas sont assez considérables, pour tenir place parmi les principaux revenus du Mogol. Tout ce casuel de l'Empire, égale, à peu prés, ou surpasse même les immenses richesses que l'Empereur perçoit des seuls fonds de terre de son Domaine. On est étonné sans doute d'une si prodigieuse opulence; mais il faut considérer que tant de richesses n'entre dans les trésors du Mogol, que pour en sortir tous les ans, du moins en partie, & pour couler une autre fois sur ses terres. La moitié de l'Empire subsiste par les libéralitez du Prince, ou du moins elle est à ses gages. Outre ce grande nombre d'Officers & de Soldats qui ne vivent que de la paye, tous les Paisans de la campagne, qui ne labourent que pour le Souverain, sont nourris à ses frais, & presque tous les Artisans des villes, qu'on fait travailler pour le Mogol, sont païez du Trésor Impérial. On conjecture assez quelle est la dépendance des Sujets, & par conséquent quelle est leur déférence pour leur Maître."

My concluding extract is taken from Harris's Voyages, wherein explanations are given in regard to the authenticity of the statistical return, and its verification from independent documents.[1] The return itself is of considerable value in this inquiry, in so distinctly supporting, in properly modified terms, the parallel list of provincial revenues furnished by Manucci. It will be seen to reproduce, in identical figures, many of the totals given in the parallel lists derived from the *Dastúr al 'Amals*, quoted at pp. 42, 43. It wisely discriminates the altered condition of Aurangzéb's kingdom in his later years, and the contrast may be followed from the minor reductions under Berár and Ahmadnagar to the more important defalcations in Bidar and Bíjápúr. As regards Manucci's returns, it lends no countenance to the introduction of an independent *Ṣúbah* under Rájmahál, and properly brings back Bengal to sober revenue proportions, from the possibly momentary receipt of the large sum placed to its credit by the Italian physician; and, further, it marks by the omission of Baglána and Nandair, and the extinction of the dubious tribute of the Mahrattas. The introductory quotation is continued from the passage reproduced in illustration of the return at page 32.

"In the latter end of his father's time, the three provinces of Balkh, Kandahár, and Badakhshán were lost, which produced a revenue of £600,000; and yet, at his decease, he left his dominions in a better condition than he found them, as will appear from the following succinct table of provinces and their revenues, which may be depended upon, and which will be of great use in understanding the subsequent part of this

[1] The chapter from which this passage is copied is headed, "Taken chiefly from the accurate edition of Ramusio, compared with an original MS. in his Prussian Majesty's Library, and with most of the translations hitherto published."

work, as well as other books which treat of the Mogul Empire."

AURANGZÉB'S REVENUES IN 1707.

19 Old Ṣúbahs (Provinces).

	Dáms.		Rupees.
1. Dehli	122,19,50,137	=	3,05,48,753
2. Agrah	114,67,60,157		2,86,69,003
3. Ajmír	65,23,45,362		1,63,08,634
4. Allahábád	45,65,43,248		1,14,13,581
5. Punjáb	82,61,32,107		2,06,53,302
6. Oude	32,23,27,829		80,58,195
7. Multán	21,44,42,936		53,61,073
8. Kábul	16,10,39,354		40,25,983
9. Kashmír	22,99,11,397		57,47,734
10. Gujarát	60,78,49,135		1,51.96,228
11. Bihár	40,71,61,000		1,01,79,025
12. Sind	9,18,16,810		22,95,420
13. Daulatábád	103,49,45,100		2,58,73,627
14. Málwah	40,39,01,658		1,00,97,541
15. Berár	61,40,25,000		1,53,50,625
16. Khándés	44,86,30,000		1,12,15,750
17. Bidar	37,29,74,370		93,24,359
18. Bengal	52,46,36,240		1,31,15,906
19. Orissa	14,28,20,000		35,70,500
The two New Ṣúbahs.			
20. Haidarábád	111,33,60,000		2,78,34,000
21. Bíjápúr	107,83,05,000		2,69,57,625
	1207,18,76,840	=	30,17,96,864

The equivalent sum total given in the text is £37,724,615, but the aggregate items do not make more than £30,179,692.[1] The difference, as is obvious, having arisen from the authors allowing 2*s*. 6*d*. for the exchange rate of the rupee (or 1000 rupees = £125); whereas, throughout these calculations, the *nominal* exchange has been reduced to the conventional *even* sum of 2*s*. per rupee, or 10 rupees to the £ sterling, which, though it accords more closely with modern exchanges, and is especially simple in its exhibition of comparative ratios, can scarcely be said to have represented the true equivalent, or purchasing power of the current coin of the period, so well as the practical illustration given by the contemporary observer.

Finally, to recapitulate the data collected in the previous pages, I have cast the leading results into tabular forms, the one exhibiting the contrasted provincial returns, the other giving at one view the variations of the grand totals of the revenue of the Mughals for 113 years.

The former furnishes a curious chart of the changing boundaries of the empire—a faithful index of the agricultural advance or retrogression of the several provinces, and suggestive evidence of the effect of the residence of the Court upon the material prosperity of the favoured locality.

The second table instructs us as to what the magnificent domain we now administer could then pay with but little effort, and under many adverse influences.

[1] 1207,18,76,840 ÷ 40 = 301,79,69,840 ÷ 10 = £30,179,926.

Contrasted Returns of the Provincial Revenues of the Mughal Empire at Various Periods (In Rupees).

	A.D. 1594. Akbar.	A.D. 1648. Sháh Jahán.	A.D. 1654. Aurangzéb.	A.D. 1663–66 ? Bernier's return.	Date uncertain. Official returns.	A.D. 1697. Aurangzéb.	A.D. 1707. Aurangzéb.
1. Allahábád...	53,10,677	1,00,00,000	1,31,97,029	94,70,000	1,14,13,575	77,38,000	1,14,13,581
2. Agrah	1,36,56,257	2,25,00,000	3,41,15,052	2,52,25,000	2,85,44,003	2,22,03,550	2,86,69,003
3. Oude.........	50,43,954	75,00,000	90,99,571	68,30,000	80,32,927	. . .	80,58,195
4. Ajmír	71,53,449	1,50,00,000	1,62,19,042	2,19,70,000	1,63,08,642	2,19,00,002	1,63,08,634
5. Gujarát......	1,09,24,122	1,32,50,000	2,17,32,201	1,33,95,000	1,13,68,728	2,33,05,000	1,51,96,228
6. Bihár.........	55,47,985	1,00,00,000	1,36,32,523	95,80,000	1,01,79,525	1,21,50,000	1,01,79,025
7. Bengal	1,49,61,482	1,25,00,000	1,14,46,450	. . .	1,31,15,906	4,00,00,000	1,31,15,906
8. Dehli.........	1,50,40,388	2,50,00,000	3,89,70,978	1,95,25,000	3,03,23,753	1,25,50,000	3,05,48,753
9. Kábul	80,71,024	40,00,000	24,26,950	32,72,500	40,25,983	32,07,250	40,25,983
10. Láhor	1,39,86,460	2,25,00,000	2,72,43,994	2,46,95,000	2,24,53,302	2,33,95,000	2,06,53,302
11. Multán	96,00,764	70,00,000	84,60,529	1,18,40,500	53,57,500	50,25,000	53,61,073
12. Málwah......	60,17,376	1,00,00,000	1,39,32,933	91,62,500	1,00,99,516	99,06,250	1,00,97,541
13. Berár.........	1,73,76,117	1,37,50,000	1,47,65,000	1,58,75,000	2,72,93,131	1,58,07,500	1,53,50,625

14. Khándés ...	75,63,237	1,00,00,000	1,24,23,250	1,85,50,000	1,48,23,308	1,11,05,000	1,12,15,750
15. Ahmadnagar (Daulatábád)	(No return)	1,37,50,000	1,26,79,000	1,72,27,500	3,50,71,119	a. 1,62,04,750 c. 2,00,00,000	2,58,73,622
16. Taṭah	16,56,284	20,00,000	22,30,750	23,20,000	17,20,420	60,02,000	22,95,420
17. Bakar	. . .	. . .	. . .	. . .	. . .	24,00,000	
18. Ḳandahár ...	. . .	15,00,000	15,00,000	19,92,500			
19. Badakhshán.	. . .	10,00,000					
20. Baglánah ...	. . .	5,00,000	. . .	5,00,000	. . .	68,85,000 b. 72,00,000	
21. Balkh	. . .	20,00,000					
22. Kashmír ...	. . .	37,50,000	28,59,750	3,50,000	57,47,509	35,05,000	57,47,734
23. Orissa	. . .	50,00,000	56,39,500	72,70,000	35,58,025	57,07,500	35,70,500
24. Rájmahál ...	. . .	. . .	. . .	. . .	. . .	1,00,50,000	
25. Telingána ... (Haiderábád, Golconda.)	. . .	75,00,000	48,65,200	68,85,000	2,73,38,200	5,00,00,000	2,78,34,000
26. Bidar	. . .	. . .	. . .	. . .	1,32,68,558	. . .	93,24,359
27. Bíjápúr	. . .	. . .	. . .	. . .	5,63,70,678	5,00,00,000	2,69,57,625
Rupees,	14,19,09,576	22,00,00,000	26,74,39,702	22,59,35,500	35,64,14,308	38,62,46,802	30,17,96,859

Recapitulation of the Amount of the Revenues of the Mughal Empire at Various Periods, Rejecting all Imperfect Returns.

Mughal Emperors.	Authority.	Land Revenue.	Revenue from all sources.
1. Akbar, A.D. 1593	Nizám-ud-dín Ahmad		£ 32,000,000
2. ,, A.D. 1594	Abúl Fazl, MSS.	£ 16,574,388	
3. ,, ,,	Official documents	16,582,440	
4. ,, A.D. 1605	Indian authorities, quoted by De Laët	17,450,000	
5. Jahángír, A.D. 1609–11	Captain W. Hawkins		50,000,000
6. ,, A.D. 1628	Abd ul Hamíd Láhóri	17,500,000	
7. Sháh Jahán, A.D. 1648–9	Ditto	22,000,000	
8. Aurangzéb, A.D. 1655	Official documents	Gross, 26,743,970 Nett, 24,056,114	
9. ,,	Later official documents	Gross, 35,641,431 Nett, 34,505,890	
10. ,, A.D. 1695	Gemelli Careri		80,000,000
11. ,, A.D. 1697	Mannucci (Catrou)	38,719,400 × 2 =	77,438,800
12. ,, A.D. 1707	Ramusio	30,179,692	

A LIST

OF

NEW AND IMPORTANT PUBLICATIONS

OF

MESSRS. TRÜBNER & CO., LONDON.

Alabaster.—The Wheel of the Law: Buddhism illustrated from Siamese Sources by the Modern Buddhist, a Life of Buddha, and an account of the Phra Bat. By Henry Alabaster, Esq., Interpreter of Her Majesty's Consulate-General in Siam; Member of the Royal Asiatic Society. Demy 8vo. pp. lviii. and 324. 1871. (14*s.*) Rs. 7.

Beal.—A Catena of Buddhist Scriptures from the Chinese. By S. Beal, B.A., Trinity College, Cambridge; a Chaplain in Her Majesty's Fleet, etc. 8vo. cloth, pp. xiv. and 436. 1871. (15*s.*) Rs. 7, 8 As.

Buddhaghosha.—Buddhaghosha's Parables: translated from Burmese by Captain H. T. Rogers, R.E. With an Introduction containing Buddha's Dhammapadam, or, Path of Virtue; translated from Pali by F. Max Müller. 8vo. pp. 378, cloth. (12*s.* 6*d.*) Rs. 6, 4 As.

CUNNINGHAM.—The Ancient Geography of India. I. The Buddhist Period, including the Campaigns of Alexander, and the Travels of Hwen-Thsang. By Alexander Cunningham, Major-General, Royal Engineers (Bengal Retired). With thirteen Maps. 8vo. pp. xx. and 590, cloth. 1870. (28s.) Rs. 14.

Elliot.—The History of India, as told by its own Historians. The Muhammadan Period. Edited from the Posthumous Papers of the late Sir H. M. Elliot, K.C.B., East India Company's Bengal Civil Service, by Prof. John Dowson, M.R.A.S., Staff College, Sandhurst. Vols. I. and II. With a Portrait of Sir H. M. Elliot. 8vo. pp xxxii. and 542, x. and 580, cloth. (18*s.* each.) Rs., 9 each. Vol. III. 8vo. pp. xii. and 627, cloth. (24*s.*) Rs. 12.

Elliot.—Memoirs on the History, Folklore, and Distribution of the Races of the North Western Provinces of India; being an amplified Edition of the original Supplementary Glossary of Indian Terms. By the late Sir Henry M. Elliot, K.C.B., of the Hon. East India Company's Bengal Civil Service. Edited, revised, and re-arranged, by John Beames, M.R.A.S., Bengal Civil Service; Member of the German Oriental Society, of the Asiatic Societies of Paris and Bengal, and of the Philological Society of London. In 2 vols. demy 8vo., pp. xx., 370, and 396, cloth. With two Lithographic Plates, one full-page coloured Map, and three large coloured folding Maps. (36*s.*) Rs. 18.

Ikhwánu-s Safá.—Ikhwánu-s Safá; or, Brothers of Purity. Describing the Contention between Men and Beasts as to the Superiority of the Human Race. Translated from the Hindustání by Professor J. Dowson, Staff College, Sandhurst. Crown 8vo. pp. viii. and 156, cloth. (7*s.*) Rs. 3, 8 As.

Khirad-Afroz (The Illuminator of the Understanding). By Maulaví Hafízu'd-dín. A new edition of the Hindústání Text, carefully revised, with Notes, Critical and Explanatory. By Edward B. Eastwick, M.P., F.R.S., F.S.A., M.R.A.S., Professor of Hindústání at the late East India Company's College at Haileybury. 8vo. cloth, pp. xiv. and 321. (18*s.*) Rs. 9.

Kistner.—Buddha and his Doctrines. A Bibliographical Essay. By Otto Kistner. Imperial 8vo., pp. iv. and 32, sewed. (2*s.* 6*d.*) R. 1, 4 As.

MAHA-VIRA-CHARITA; or, the Adventures of the Great Hero Rama. An Indian Drama in Seven Acts. Translated into English Prose from the Sanskrit of Bhavabhûti. By John Pickford, M.A. Crown 8vo cloth, pp. xx. and 172. (5s.) Rs. 2, 8 As.

Megha-Duta (The). (Cloud Messenger.) By Kálídása. Translated from the Sanskrit into English verse, with Notes and Illustrations, by the late H. H. Wilson, M.A., F.R.S., Boden Professor of Sanskrit in the University of Oxford, etc., etc. The Vocabulary by Francis Johnson, some time Professor of Oriental Languages at the College of the Honourable the East India Company, Haileybury. New edition. 4to. cloth, pp. xi. and 180. (10*s.* 6*d.*) Rs. 5, 4 As.

Muir.—Original Sanskrit Texts, on the Origin and History of the People of India, their Religion and Institutions. Collected, Translated, and Illustrated by John Muir, Esq., D.C.L., LL.D., Ph.D.

Second Edition. Vol. II. 8vo. pp. xxxii., 512. 1872. (21*s.*) Rs. 10, 8 As.

Müller (Max).—The Sacred Hymns of the Brahmins, as preserved to us in the oldest collection of religious poetry, the Rig-Veda-Sanhita, translated and explained. By F. Max Müller, M.A., Fellow of All Souls' College; Professor of Comparative Philology at Oxford; Foreign Member of the Institute of France, etc., etc. In 8 vols. Volume I. 8vo. pp. clii. and 264. (12*s.* 6*d.*) Rs. 6, 4 As.

Ram Raz.—Essay on the Architecture of the Hindus. By Ram Raz, Native Judge and Magistrate of Bangalore, Corresponding Member of the R.A.S. of Great Britain and Ireland. With 48 plates. 4to. pp. xiv. and 64, sewed. London, 1834. Original selling price, £1 11*s.* 6*d.*, reduced (for a short time) to (12*s.*) Rs. 6.

Sherring.—The Sacred City of the Hindus. An Account of Benares in Ancient and Modern Times. By the Rev. M. A. Sherring, M.A., LL.D.; and Prefaced with an Introduction by Fitz-Edward Hall, Esq., D.C.L. 8vo. cloth, pp. xxxvi. and 388, with numerous full-page Illustrations. (21*s.*) Rs. 10, 8 As.

Thomas.—Early Sassanian Inscriptions, Seals and Coins, illustrating the Early History of the Sassanian Dynasty, containing Proclamations of Ardeshir Babek, Sapor I., and his Successors. With a Critical Examination and Explanation of the Celebrated Inscription in the Hájíábad Cave, demonstrating that Sapor, the Conqueror of Valerian, was a Professing Christian. By Edward Thomas, Esq. Illustrated. 8vo. cloth, pp. 148. (7*s.* 6*d.*) Rs. 3, 12 As.

THOMAS.—The Chronicles of the Pathán Kings of Dehli. Illustrated by Coins, Inscriptions, and other Antiquarian Remains. By Edward Thomas, F.R.S., F.R.A.S., late of the East India Company's Bengal Civil Service. With numerous Copperplates and Woodcuts. Demy 8vo. cloth, pp. xxiv. and 467. 1871. (28s.) Rs. 14.

Vishnu-Purana (The); a System of Hindu Mythology and Tradition. Translated from the original Sanskrit, and Illustrated by Notes derived chiefly from other Purāṇas. By the late H. H. Wilson, M.A., F.R.S., Boden Professor of Sanskrit in the University of Oxford, etc., etc. Edited by Fitzedward Hall. In 6 vols. 8vo. Vol. I. pp. cxl. and 200; Vol. II. pp. 343; Vol. III. pp. 348; Vol. IV. pp. 346, cloth; Vol. V. pp. 392, cloth. (Price 10*s.* 6*d.* each). Rs. 5, 4 As. each. [*Vol. VI. in preparation.*

Wheeler.—The History of India from the Earliest Ages. By J. Talboys Wheeler, Assistant Secretary to the Government of India in the Foreign Department, Secretary to the Indian Record Commission, author of "The Geography of Herodotus," etc. etc. Vol. I., The Vedic Period and the Maha Bharata. 8vo. cloth, pp. lxxv. and 576. (18*s.*) Rs. 9.

Vol. II., The Ramayana and the Brahmanic Period. 8vo. cloth, pp. lxxxviii. and 680, with 2 Maps. (21*s.*) Rs. 10, 8 As.

WILSON.—Select Specimens of the Theatre of the Hindus. By the late Horace Hayman Wilson. Third corrected Edition. In 2 vols. demy 8vo. cloth. (Price 21s.) Rs. 10, As. 8.

STEPHEN AUSTIN AND SONS PRINTERS, HERTFORD.

LINGUISTIC PUBLICATIONS

OF

TRÜBNER & CO.,

8 AND 60, PATERNOSTER ROW, LONDON, E.C.

Ahlwardt.—THE DIVÁNS OF THE SIX ANCIENT ARABIC POETS, Ennábiga, 'Antara, Tarafa, Zuhair, 'Algama, and Imruolgais; chiefly according to the MSS. of Paris, Gotha, and Leyden, and the collection of their Fragments: with a complete list of the various readings of the Text. Edited by W. AHLWARDT, Professor of Oriental Languages at the University of Geifswald. 8vo. pp. xxx. 340, sewed. 1870. 12*s.*

Aitareya Brahmanam of the Rig Veda. 2 vols. See under HAUG.

Alabaster.—THE WHEEL OF THE LAW: Buddhism illustrated from Siamese Sources by the Modern Buddhist, a Life of Buddha, and an account of the Phra Bat. By HENRY ALABASTER, Esq., Interpreter of Her Majesty's Consulate-General in Siam; Member of the Royal Asiatic Society. Demy 8vo. pp. lviii. and 324. 1871. 14*s.*

Alcock.—A PRACTICAL GRAMMAR of the JAPANESE LANGUAGE. By Sir RUTHERFORD ALCOCK, Resident British Minister at Jeddo. 4to. pp. 61 sewed. 18*s.*

Alcock.—FAMILIAR DIALOGUES in JAPANESE, with English and French Translations, for the use of Students. By Sir RUTHERFORD ALCOCK. 8vo. pp. viii. and 40, sewed. Paris and London, 1863. 5*s.*

Alger.—THE POETRY OF THE ORIENT. By WILLIAM ROUNSEVILLE ALGER, 8vo. cloth, pp. xii. and 337. 9*s.*

Alif Laîlat wa Laîlat.—THE ARABIAN NIGHTS. 4 vols. 4to. pp. 495, 493, 442, 434. Cairo, A.H. 1279 (1862). £3 3*s.*

This celebrated Edition of the Arabian Nights is now, for the first time, offered at a price which makes it accessible to Scholars of limited means.

Andrews.—A DICTIONARY OF THE HAWAIIAN LANGUAGE, to which is appended an English-Hawaiian Vocabulary, and a Chronological Table of Remarkable Events. By LORRIN ANDREWS. 8vo. pp. 560, cloth. £1 11*s.* 6*d.*

Anthropological Institute of Great Britain and Ireland (The Journal of the). Sir JOHN LUBBOCK, Bart., M.P., F.R.S., President. Published Quarterly.

Vol I., No. 1. January-July, 1871. 8vo. pp. 120–clix, sewed. Illustrated with 11 full page Plates, and numerous Woodcuts; and accompanied by several folding plates of Tables, etc. 7*s.*

CONTENTS.—On the Development of Relationships. By Sir John Lubbock, Bart., M.P., F.R.S., President A.I.—On the Racial Aspect of the Franco-Prussian War. By J. W. Jackson, Esq., M.A.I.—On the Pre-historic and Proto-historic Relations of the Populations of Asia and Europe, in reference to Palæo-Asiatic, Caucaso-Tibetan, Palæo-Georgian, &c. By Hyde Clarke, Esq.—Report on the Results obtained by the Settle Cave Exploration Committee out of Victoria Cave in 1870 (with 2 plates).—The Builders of the Megalithic Monuments of Britain. By A. L. Lewis, Esq., M.A.I.—The Mental Characteristics of Primitive Man as exemplified by the Australian Aborigines. By C. L. Wake, Esq., Dir. A.I.—Notes on a Comparative Table of the Australian Languages. By the Rev. G. Taplin (with folding tables).—On the Position of the Australian Languages. By W. H. I. Bleek, Esq., Ph. D.

APPENDIX.—A Description of some Archaic Structures in Cornwall and Devon. By A. L. Lewis, Esq., F.A.S.L.—Some Objections to the Theory of Natural Selections as explained by Mr. A. R. Wallace. By Henry Muirhead, Esq., M.D.

500.

8 9 72

Vol. I., No. 2. October, 1871. 8vo. pp. 121–264, sewed. 4*s.*

CONTENTS.—On the Stone Monuments of the Khâsi Hill Tribes, and on some of the peculiar Rites and Customs of the People. By Major H. H. Godwin-Austen, F.R.G.S.—Vocabulary of the Cornu Tribe of Australia. By Dr. W. A. Pechey.—Chinese Mohammedans. By J. Anderson, Esq., M.D., F.R.S.—On Divination and Analogous Phenomena among the Natives of Natal. By Rev. Canon H. Calloway, M.D.—A Description of the Quissama Tribe. By F. G. H. Price, Esq., F.R.G.S., M.A.I.—On the Races of Patagonia. By Lieut. Musters, R.N.—On Chinese Burials. By Dr. W. Eatwell.—On the Discovery of a Cairn at Khangaum. By J. J. Carey, Esq. (communicated by Dr. A. Campbell.)—On a Cist found in Argyllshire. By Dugald Sinclair, Esq. (communicated by Dr. A. Campbell.)—On a Kitchen Midden in Cork Harbour. By G. M. Atkinson, Esq.—Mode of Preparing the Dead among the Natives of the Upper Mary River, Queensland. By A. McDonald, Esq. (communicated by W. Boyd Dawkins, Esq., F.R.S.)—On some Forms of Ancient Interment in Co. Antrim. By J. Sinclair Holden, Esq., M.D., F.G.S.—On the Analogies and Coincidences among Unconnected Nations. By H. W. Westropp, Esq.—The Westerly Drifting of Nomades from the Fifth to the Nineteenth Century. Part VI. The Kirghises or Bourouts, the Kazaks, Kalmucks, Euzbegs, and Nogays. By Henry H. Howorth, Esq.—Part VII. The Thukine or Turks Proper, and the Hoeitche or Uzes.—Anthropological Miscellanea.

Arabic, Persian, and Turkish Books (A Catalogue of). Printed in the East. Constantly for sale by Trübner and Co., 8 and 60, Paternoster Row, London. CONTENTS.—Arabic, Persian, and Turkish Books printed in Egypt.—Arabic Books printed in Oudh.—Persian Literature printed in Oudh.—Editions of the Koran printed in Oudh.—Arabic Books printed at Bombay.—Persian Books printed at Bombay.—Arabic Literature printed at Tunis.—Arabic Literature printed in Syria. 16mo. pp. 68, sewed. 1*s.*

Asher.—ON THE STUDY OF MODERN LANGUAGES IN GENERAL, and of the English Language in particular. An Essay. By DAVID ASHER, Ph.D. 12mo. pp. viii. and 80, cloth. 2*s.*

Asiatic Society.—JOURNAL OF THE ROYAL ASIATIC SOCIETY OF GREAT BRITAIN AND IRELAND, from the Commencement to 1863. First Series, complete in 20 Vols. 8vo., with many Plates. Price £10; or, in Single Numbers, as follows:—Nos. 1 to 14, 6*s.* each; No. 15, 2 Parts, 4*s.* each; No. 16, 2 Parts, 4*s.* each; No. 17, 2 Parts, 4*s.* each; No. 18, 6*s.* These 18 Numbers form Vols. I. to IX.—Vol. X., Part 1, op.; Part 2, 5*s.*; Part 3, 5*s.*—Vol. XI., Part 1, 6*s.*; Part 2 not published.—Vol. XII., 2 Parts, 6*s.* each.—Vol. XIII., 2 Parts, 6*s.* each.—Vol. XIV., Part 1, 5*s.*; Part 2 not published.—Vol. XV., Part 1, 6*s.*; Part 2, with Maps, 10*s.*—Vol. XVI., 2 Parts, 6*s.* each.—Vol. XVII., 2 Parts, 6*s.* each.—Vol. XVIII., 2 Parts, 6*s.* each.—Vol. XIX., Parts 1 to 4, 16*s.*—Vol. XX., 3 Parts, 4*s.* each.

Asiatic Society.—JOURNAL OF THE ROYAL ASIATIC SOCIETY OF GREAT BRITAIN AND IRELAND. *New Series.* Vol. I. In Two Parts. pp. iv. and 490, sewed. 16*s.*

CONTENTS.—I. Vajra-chhedikâ, the "Kin Kong King," or Diamond Sûtra. Translated from the Chinese by the Rev. S. Beal, Chaplain, R.N.—II. The Pâramitâ-hridaya Sûtra, or, in Chinese, "Mo-ho-pô-ye-po-lo-mih-to-sin-king," *i.e.* "The Great Pâramitâ Heart Sûtra." Translated from the Chinese by the Rev. S. Beal, Chaplain, R.N.—III. On the Preservation of National Literature in the East. By Colonel F. J. Goldsmid.—IV. On the Agricultural, Commercial, Financial, and Military Statistics of Ceylon. By E. R. Power, Esq.—V. Contributions to a Knowledge of the Vedic Theogony and Mythology. By J. Muir, D.C.L., LL.D.—VI. A Tabular List of Original Works and Translations, published by the late Dutch Government of Ceylon at their Printing Press at Colombo. Compiled by Mr. Mat. P. J. Ondaatje, of Colombo.—VII. Assyrian and Hebrew Chronology compared, with a view of showing the extent to which the Hebrew Chronology of Ussher must be modified, in conformity with the Assyrian Canon. By J. W. Bosanquet, Esq.—VIII. On the existing Dictionaries of the Malay Language. By Dr. H. N. van der Tuuk.—IX. Bilingual Readings: Cuneiform and Phœnician. Notes on some Tablets in the British Museum, containing Bilingual Legends (Assyrian and Phœnician). By Major-General Sir H. Rawlinson, K.C.B., Director R.A.S.—X. Translations of Three Copper-plate Inscriptions of the Fourth Century A.D., and Notices of the Châlukya and Gurjjara Dynasties By Professor J. Dowson, Staff College, Sandhurst.—XI. Yama and the Doctrine of a Future Life, according to the Rig-Yajur-, and Atharva-Vedas. By J. Muir, Esq., D.C.L., LL.D.—XII. On the Jyotisha Observation of the Place of the Colures, and the Date derivable from it. By William D. Whitney, Esq., Professor of Sanskrit in Yale College, New Haven, U.S.—Note on the preceding Article. By Sir Edward Colebrooke, Bart., M.P., President R.A.S.—XIII. Progress of the Vedic Religion towards Abstract Conceptions of the Deity. By J. Muir, Esq., D.C.L., LL.D.—XIV. Brief Notes on the Age and Authenticity of the Work of Aryabhata, Varâhamihira, Brahmagupta, Bhattotpala, and Bhâskarâchârya. By Dr. Bhâu Dâjî, Honorary Member R.A.S.—XV. Outlines of a Grammar of the Malagasy Language. By H. N. Van der Tuuk.—XVI. On the Identity of Xandrames and Krananda. By Edward Thomas, Esq.

Vol. II. In Two Parts. pp. 522, sewed. 16*s*.

CONTENTS.—I. Contributions to a Knowledge of Vedic Theogony and Mythology. No. 2. By J. Muir, Esq.—II. Miscellaneous Hymns from the Rig- and Atharva-Vedas. By J. Muir, Esq.—III. Five hundred questions on the Social Condition of the Natives of Bengal. By the Rev. J. Long.—IV. Short account of the Malay Manuscripts belonging to the Royal Asiatic Society. By Dr. H. N. van der Tuuk.—V. Translation of the Amitâbha Sûtra from the Chinese. By the Rev. S. Beal, Chaplain Royal Navy.—VI. The initial coinage of Bengal. By Edward Thomas, Esq.—VII. Specimens of an Assyrian Dictionary. By Edwin Norris, Esq.—VIII. On the Relations of the Priests to the other classes of Indian Society in the Vedic age. By J. Muir, Esq.—IX. On the Interpretation of the Veda. By the same.—X. An attempt to Translate from the Chinese a work known as the Confessional Services of the great compassionate Kwan Yin, possessing 1000 hands and 1000 eyes. By the Rev. S. Beal, Chaplain Royal Navy. —XI. The Hymns of the Gaupâyanas and the Legend of King Asamâti. By Professor Max Müller, M.A., Honorary Member Royal Asiatic Society.—XII. Specimen Chapters of an Assyrian Grammar. By the Rev. E. Hincks, D.D., Honorary Member Royal Asiatic Society.

Vol. III. In Two Parts. pp. 516, sewed. With Photograph. 22*s*.

CONTENTS.—I. Contributions towards a Glossary of the Assyrian Language. By H. F. Talbot. —II. Remarks on the Indo-Chinese Alphabets. By Dr. A. Bastian.—III. The poetry of Mohamed Rabadan, Arragonese. By the Hon. H. E. J. Stanley.—IV. Catalogue of the Oriental Manuscripts in the Library of King's College, Cambridge. By Edward Henry Palmer, B.A., Scholar of St. John's College, Cambridge; Member of the Royal Asiatic Society; Membre de la Société Asiatique de Paris.—V. Description of the Amravati Tope in Guntur. By J. Fergusson, Esq., F.R.S.—VI. Remarks on Prof. Brockhaus' edition of the Kathâsarit-sâgara, Lambaka IX. XVIII. By Dr. H. Kern, Professor of Sanskrit in the University of Leyden.—VII. The source of Colebrooke's Essay "On the Duties of a Faithful Hindu Widow." By Fitzedward Hall, Esq., M.A., D.C.L. Oxon. Supplement: Further detail of proofs that Colebrooke's Essay, "On the Duties of a Faithful Hindu Widow," was not indebted to the Vivâdabhangârnava. By Fitzedward Hall, Esq.—VIII. The Sixth Hymn of the First Book of the Rig Veda. By Professor Max Müller, M.A., Hon. M.R.A.S.—IX. Sassanian Inscriptions. By E. Thomas, Esq.—X. Account of an Embassy from Morocco to Spain in 1690 and 1691. By the Hon. H. E. J. Stanley.—XI. The Poetry of Mohamed Rabadan, of Arragon. By the Hon. H. E. J. Stanley.—XII. Materials for the History of India for the Six Hundred Years of Mohammadan rule, previous to the Foundation of the British Indian Empire. By Major W. Nassau Lees, LL.D., Ph.D.--XIII. A Few Words concerning the Hill people inhabiting the Forests of the Cochin State. By Captain G. E. Fryer, Madras Staff Corps, M.R.A.S.—XIV. Notes on the Bhojpuri Dialect of Hindi, spoken in Western Behar. By John Beames, Esq., B.C.S., Magistrate of Chumparun.

Vol. IV. In Two Parts. pp. 521, sewed. 16*s*.

CONTENTS.—I. Contribution towards a Glossary of the Assyrian Language. By H. F. Talbot. Part II.—II. On Indian Chronology. By J. Fergusson, Esq., F.R.S.—III. The Poetry of Mohamed Rabadan of Arragon. By the Hon. H. E. J. Stanley.—IV. On the Magar Language of Nepal. By John Beames, Esq., B.C.S.—V. Contributions to the Knowledge of Parsee Literature. By Edward Sachau, Ph.D.—VI. Illustrations of the Lamaist System in Tibet, drawn from Chinese Sources. By Wm. Frederick Mayers, Esq., of H.B.M. Consular Service, China.—VII. Khuddaka Pátha, a Páli Text, with a Translation and Notes. By R. C. Childers, late of the Ceylon Civil Service.—VIII. An Endeavour to elucidate Rashiduddin's Geographical Notices of India. By Col. H. Yule, C.B.—IX. Sassanian Inscriptions explained by the Pahlavi of the Pârsis. By E. W. West, Esq.—X. Some Account of the Senbyû Pagoda at Mengûn, near the Burmese Capital, in a Memorandum by Capt. E. H. Sladan, Political Agent at Mandalé; with Remarks on the Subject by Col. Henry Yule, C.B.—XI. The Brhat-Sanhitâ; or, Complete System of Natural Astrology of Varâha-Mihira. Translated from Sanskrit into English by Dr. H. Kern.—XII. The Mohammedan Law of Evidence, and its influence on the Administration of Justice in India. By N. B. E. Baillie, Esq.—XIII. The Mohammedan Law of Evidence in connection with the Administration of Justice to Foreigners. By N. B. E. Baillie, Esq.—XIV. A Translation of a Bactrian Páli Inscription. By Prof. J. Dowson.—XV. Indo-Parthian Coins. By E. Thomas, Esq.

Vol. V. Part I. pp. 197, sewed. 8*s*.

CONTENTS.—I. Two Jâtakas. The original Páli Text, with an English Translation. By V. Fausböll.—II. On an Ancient Buddhist Inscription at Keu-yung kwan, in North China. By A. Wylie.—III. The Brhat Sanhitâ; or, Complete System of Natural Astrology of Varâha-Mihira Translated from Sanskrit into English by Dr. H. Kern.—IV. The Pongol Festival in Southern India. By Charles E. Gover.—V. The Poetry of Mohamed Rabadan, of Arragon. By the Right Hon. Lord Stanley of Alderley.—VI. Essay on the Creed and Customs of the Jangams. By Charles P. Brown.—VII. On Malabar, Coromandel, Quilon, etc. By C. P. Brown.—VIII. On the Treatment of the Nexus in the Neo-Aryan Languages of India. By John Beames, B.C.S.—IX. Some Remarks on the Great Tope at Sânchi. By the Rev. S. Beal.—X. Ancient Inscriptions from Mathura. Translated by Professor J. Dowson.—Note to the Mathura Inscriptions. By Major-General A. Cunningham.

Asiatic Society.—TRANSACTIONS OF THE ROYAL ASIATIC SOCIETY OF GREAT BRITAIN AND IRELAND. Complete in 3 vols. 4to., 80 Plates of Facsimiles, etc., cloth. London, 1827 to 1835. Published at £9 5*s*.; reduced to £3 3*s*.

The above contains contributions by Professor Wilson, G. C. Haughton, Davis, Morrison, Colebrooke, Humboldt, Dorn, Grotefend, and other eminent Oriental scholars.

Atharva Veda Práticákhya.—See under WHITNEY.

Auctores Sanscriti. Edited for the Sanskrit Text Society, under the supervision of THEODOR GOLDSTÜCKER. Vol. I., containing the Jaiminîya-Nyâya-Mâlâ-Vistara. Parts I. to V., pp. 1 to 400, large 4to. sewed. 10*s.* each part.

Axon.—THE LITERATURE OF THE LANCASHIRE DIALECT. A Bibliographical Essay. By WILLIAM E. A. AXON, F.R.S.L. Fcap. 8vo. sewed. 1870. 1*s.*

Bachmaier.—PASIGRAPHICAL DICTIONARY AND GRAMMAR. By ANTON BACHMAIER, President of the Central Pasigraphical Society at Munich. 18mo. cloth, pp. viii.; 26; 160. 1870. 3*s.* 6*d.*

Bachmaier.—PASIGRAPHISCHES WÖRTERBUCH ZUM GEBRAUCHE FÜR DIE DEUTSCHE SPRACHE. Verfasst von ANTON BACHMAIER, Vorsitzendem des Central-Vereins für Pasigraphie in München. 18mo. cloth, pp. viii.; 32; 128; 120. 1870. 2*s.* 6*d.*

Bachmaier.—DICTIONNAIRE PASIGRAPHIQUE, PRÉCEDÉ DE LA GRAMMAIRE. Redigé par ANTOINE BACHMAIER, Président de la Société Centrale de Pasigraphie à Munich. 18mo. cloth, pp. vi. 26; 168; 150. 1870. 2*s.* 6*d.*

Bálávatáro (A Translation of the). A Native Grammar of the Pali Language. See under LEE.

Ballad Society's Publications.—Subscriptions—Small paper, one guinea, and large paper, three guineas, per annum.

1868.

1. BALLADS FROM MANUSCRIPTS. Vol. I. Ballads on the condition of England in Henry VIII.'s and Edward VI.'s Reigns (including the state of the Clergy, Monks, and Friars), on Wolsey and Anne Boleyn. Part I. Edited by F. J. FURNIVALL, M.A. 8vo.

2. BALLADS FROM MANUSCRIPTS. Vol. II. Part 1. The Poore Mans Pittance. By Richard Williams. Edited by F. J. FURNIVALL, M.A. 8vo.

1869.

3. THE ROXBURGHE BALLADS. Part 1. With short Notes by W. CHAPPELL, Esq., F.S.A., author of "Popular Music of the Olden Time," etc., etc., and with copies of the Original Woodcuts, drawn by Mr. RUDOLPH BLIND and Mr. W. H. HOOPER, and engraved by Mr. J. H. RIMBAULT and Mr. HOOPER. 8vo.

1870.

4. THE ROXBURGHE BALLADS. Vol. I. Part II. With short Notes by W. CHAPPELL, Esq., F.S.A., and with copies of the Original Woodcuts, drawn by Mr. RUDOLPH BLIND and Mr. W. H. HOOPER, and engraved by Mr. J. H. RIMBAULT and Mr. HOOPER. 1871.

5. THE ROXBURGHE BALLADS. Vol. I. Part III. With an Introduction and short Notes by W. CHAPPELL, Esq., F.S.A., Author of "Popular Music of the Olden Times," etc., etc., and with Copies of the Original Woodcuts drawn by Mr. RUDOLPH BLIND and Mr. W. H. HOOPER, and engraved by Mr. J. H. RIMBAULT and Mr. HOOPER.

6. CAPTAIN COX, HIS BALLADS AND BOOKS; or, ROBERT LANEHAM'S Letter: Whearin part of the entertainment untoo the Queen's Majesty at Kellingworth Castl, in Warwik Sheer in this Soomez Progress, 1575, is signified; from a freend Officer attendant in the Court, unto his freend, a Citizen and Merchant of London. Re-edited, with Forewords describing all the accessible Books, Tales, and Ballads in Captain Cox's List, and the COMPLAYNT OF SCOTLAND, 1548–9 A.D. By F. J. FURNIVVLL, M.A., Cambs.

Ballantyne.—ELEMENTS OF HINDÍ AND BRAJ BHÁKÁ GRAMMAR. By the late JAMES R. BALLANTYNE, LL.D. Second edition, revised and corrected Crown 8vo., pp. 44, cloth. 5*s.*

Ballantyne.—FIRST LESSONS IN SANSKRIT GRAMMAR; together with an Introduction to the Hitopadésa. Second edition. By JAMES R. BALLANTYNE. LL.D., Librarian of the India Office. 8vo. pp. viii. and 110, cloth. 1869. 5*s.*

Bartlett.—DICTIONARY OF AMERICANISMS: a Glossary of Words and Phrases colloquially used in the United States. By JOHN R. BARTLETT. Second Edition, considerably enlarged and improved. 1 vol. 8vo., pp. xxxii. and 524, cloth. 16*s.*

Beal.—TRAVELS OF FAH HIAN AND SUNG-YUN, Buddhist Pilgrims from China to India (400 A.D. and 518 A.D.) Translated from the Chinese, by S. BEAL (B.A. Trinity College, Cambridge), a Chaplain in Her Majesty's Fleet, a Member of the Royal Asiatic Society, and Author of a Translation of the Pratimôksha and the Amithâba Sûtra from the Chinese. Crown 8vo. pp. lxxiii. and 210, cloth, ornamental, with a coloured map. 10*s.* 6*d.*

Beal.—A CATENA OF BUDDHIST SCRIPTURES FROM THE CHINESE. By S. BEAL, B.A., Trinity College, Cambridge; a Chaplain in Her Majesty's Fleet, etc. 8vo. cloth, pp. xiv. and 436. 1871. 15*s.*

Beames.—OUTLINES OF INDIAN PHILOLOGY. With a Map, showing the Distribution of the Indian Languages. By JOHN BEAMES. Second enlarged and revised edition. Crown 8vo. cloth, pp. viii. and 96. 5*s.*

Beames.—NOTES ON THE BHOJPURÍ DIALECT OF HINDÍ, spoken in Western Behar. By JOHN BEAMES, Esq., B.C.S., Magistrate of Chumparun. 8vo. pp. 26, sewed. 1868. 1*s.* 6*d.*

Beames.—A COMPARATIVE GRAMMAR OF THE MODERN ARYAN LANGUAGES OF INDIA (to wit), Hindi, Panjabi, Sindhi, Gujarati, Marathi, Uriya, and Bengali. By JOHN BEAMES, Bengal C.S., M.R.A.S., &c. [*In preparation.*

Bell.—ENGLISH VISIBLE SPEECH FOR THE MILLION, for communicating the Exact Pronunciation of the Language to Native or Foreign Learners, and for Teaching Children and illiterate Adults to Read in few Days. By ALEXANDER MELVILLE BELL, F.E.I.S., F.R.S.S.A., Lecturer on Elocution in University College, London. 4to. sewed, pp. 16. 1*s.*

Bell.—VISIBLE SPEECH; the Science of Universal Alphabetics, or Self-Interpreting Physiological Letters, for the Writing of all Languages in one Alphabet. Illustrated by Tables, Diagrams, and Examples. By ALEXANDER MELVILLE BELL, F.E.I.S., F.R.S.A., Professor of Vocal Physiology, etc. 4to., pp. 156, cloth. 15*s.*

Bellew.—A DICTIONARY OF THE PUKKHTO, OR PUKSHTO LANGUAGE, on a New and Improved System. With a reversed Part, or English and Pukkhto. By H. W. BELLEW, Assistant Surgeon, Bengal Army. Super Royal 8vo., pp. xii. and 356, cloth. 42*s.*

Bellew.—A GRAMMAR OF THE PUKKHTO OR PUKSHTO LANGUAGE, on a New and Improved System. Combining Brevity with Utility, and Illustrated by Exercises and Dialogues. By H. W. BELLEW, Assistant Surgeon, Bengal Army. Super-royal 8vo., pp. xii. and 156, cloth. 21*s.*

Bellows.—ENGLISH OUTLINE VOCABULARY, for the use of Students of the Chinese, Japanese, and other Languages. Arranged by JOHN BELLOWS. With Notes on the writing of Chinese with Roman Letters. By Professor SUMMERS, King's College, London. Crown 8vo., pp. 6 and 368, cloth. 6*s.*

Bellows.—OUTLINE DICTIONARY, FOR THE USE OF MISSIONARIES, Explorers, and Students of Language. By MAX MÜLLER, M.A., Taylorian Professor in the University of Oxford. With an Introduction on the proper use of the ordinary English Alphabet in transcribing Foreign Languages. The Vocabulary compiled by JOHN BELLOWS. Crown 8vo. Limp morocco, pp. xxxi. and 368. 7*s.* 6*d.*

Benfey.—A GRAMMAR OF THE LANGUAGE OF THE VEDAS. By Dr. THEODOR BENFEY. In 1 vol. 8vo., of about 650 pages. [*In preparation.*

Benfey.—A PRACTICAL GRAMMAR OF THE SANSKRIT LANGUAGE, for the use of Early Students. By THEODOR BENFEY, Professor of Sanskrit in the University of Göttingen. Second, revised and enlarged, edition. Royal 8vo. pp. viii. and 296, cloth. 10*s*. 6*d*.

Beurmann.—VOCABULARY OF THE TIGRÉ LANGUAGE. Written down by MORITZ VON BEURMANN. Published with a Grammatical Sketch. By Dr. A. MERX, of the University of Jena. pp. viii. and 78, cloth. 3*s*. 6*d*.

Bhagavat-Geeta.—See under WILKINS.

Bholanauth Chunder.—THE TRAVELS OF A HINDOO TO VARIOUS PARTS OF BENGAL and Upper India. By BHOLANAUTH CHUNDER, Member of the Asiatic Society of Bengal. With an Introduction by J. Talboys Wheeler, Esq., Author of "The History of India." Dedicated, by permission, to His Excellency Sir John Laird Mair Lawrence, G.C.B., G.C.S.I., Viceroy and Governor-General of India, tc. In 2 volumes, crown 8vo., cloth, pp. xxv. and 440, viii. and 410. 21*s*.

Bibliotheca Hispano-Americana. A Catalogue of SPANISH BOOKS printed in Mexico, Guatemala, Honduras, The Antilles, Venezuela, Columbia, Ecuador, Peru, Chili, Uraguay, and the Argentine Republic; and of Portuguese Books printed in Brazil. Followed by a Collection of WORKS ON THE ABORIGINAL LANGUAGES OF AMERICA. On sale at the affixed prices, by Trübner & Co., 8 and 60, Paternoster Row. Fcap. 8vo. pp. 184, sewed. 1870. 1*s*. 6*d*.

Bigandet.—THE LIFE OR LEGEND OF GAUDAMA, the Buddha of the Burmese, with Annotations. The ways to Neibban, and Notice on the Phongyies, or Burmese Monks. By the Right Reverend P. BIGANDET, Bishop of Ramatha, Vicar Apostolic of Ava and Pegu. 8vo. sewed, pp. xi., 538, and v. 18*s*.

Bleek.—A COMPARATIVE GRAMMAR OF SOUTH AFRICAN LANGUAGES. By W. H. I. BLEEK, Ph.D. Volume I. I. Phonology. II. The Concord. Section 1. The Noun. 8vo. pp. xxxvi. and 322, cloth. 16*s*.

Bleek.—REYNARD IN SOUTH AFRICA; or, Hottentot Fables. Translated from the Original Manuscript in Sir George Grey's Library. By Dr. W. H. I. BLEEK, Librarian to the Grey Library, Cape Town, Cape of Good Hope. In one volume, small 8vo., pp. xxxi. and 94, cloth. 3*s*. 6*d*.

Bombay Sanskrit Series. Edited under the superintendence of G. BÜHLER, Ph. D., Professor of Oriental Languages, Elphinstone College, and F. KIELHORN, Ph. D., Superintendent of Sanskrit Studies, Deccan College.

Already published.

1. PANCHATANTRA IV. AND V. Edited, with Notes, by G. BÜHLER, Ph. D. Pp. 84, 16. 4*s*. 6*d*.
2. NÁGOJÍBHAṬṬA'S PARIBHÁSHENDUŚEKHARA. Edited and explained by F. KIELHORN, Ph. D. Part I., the Sanskrit Text and various readings. pp. 116. 8*s*. 6*d*.
3. PANCHATANTRA II. AND III. Edited, with Notes, by G. BÜHLER, Ph. D. Pp. 86, 14, 2. 5*s*. 6*d*.
4. PANCHATANTRA I. Edited, with Notes, by F. KIELHORN, Ph.D. Pp. 114, 53. 6*s*. 6*d*.
5. KÁLIDÁSA'S RAGHUVAṂŚA. With the Commentary of Mallinátha. Edited, with Notes, by SHANKAR P. PAṆḌIT, M.A. Part I. Cantos I.-VI. 9*s*.
6. KÁLIDÁSA'S MÁLAVIKÁGNIMITRA. Edited, with Notes, by SHANKAR P. PAṆḌIT, M.A. 8*s*.
7. NÁGOJÍBHAṬṬA'S PARIBHÁSHENDUŚEKHARA Edited and explained by F. KIELHORN, Ph.D. Part II. Translation and Notes. (Paribhâshâs, i.-xxxvii.) pp. 184. 8*s*.

Bottrell.—TRADITIONS AND HEARTHSIDE STORIES OF WEST CORNWALL. By WILLIAM BOTTRELL (an old Celt). Demy 12mo. pp. vi. 292, cloth. 1870. 6*s.*

Boyce.—A GRAMMAR OF THE KAFFIR LANGUAGE.— By WILLIAM B. BOYES, Wesleyan Missionary. Third Edition, augmented and improved, with Exercises, by WILLIAM J. DAVIS, Wesleyan Missionary. 12mo. pp. xii. and 164, cloth. 8*s.*

Bowditch.—SUFFOLK SURNAMES. By N. I. BOWDITCH. Third Edition, 8vo. pp. xxvi. and 758, cloth. 7*s.* 6*d.*

Bretschneider. — ON THE KNOWLEDGE POSSESSED BY THE ANCIENT CHINESE OF THE ARABS AND ARABIAN COLONIES, and other Western Countries mentioned in Chinese Books. By E. BRETSCHNEIDER, M.D., Physician of the Russian Legation at Peking. 8vo. pp. 28, sewed. 1871. 1*s.*

Brhat-Sanhita (The).—See under Kern.

Brice.—A ROMANIZED HINDUSTANI AND ENGLISH DICTIONARY. Designed for the use of Schools and for Vernacular Students of the Language. Compiled by NATHANIEL BRICE. New Edition, Revised and Enlarged. Post 8vo. cloth, pp. vi. and 357. 8*s.*

Brinton.—THE MYTHS OF THE NEW WORLD. A Treatise on the Symbolism and Mythology of the Red Races of America. By DANIEL G. BRINTON, A.M., M.D. Crown 8vo. cloth, pp. viii. and 308. 10*s.* 6*d.*

Brown.—THE DERVISHES; or, ORIENTAL SPIRITUALISM. By JOHN P. BROWN, Secretary and Dragoman of the Legation of the United States of America at Constantinople. With twenty-four Illustrations. 8vo. cloth, pp. viii. and 415. 14*s.*

Brown.— CARNATIC CHRONOLOGY. The Hindu and Mahomedan Methods of Reckoning Time explained: with Essays on the Systems; Symbols used for Numerals, a new Titular Method of Memory, Historical Records, and other subjects. By CHARLES PHILIP BROWN, Member of the Royal Asiatic Society; late of the Madras Civil Service; Telugu Translator to Government; Senior Member of the College Board, etc.; Author of the Telugu Dictionaries and Grammar, etc. 4to. sewed, pp. xii. and 90. 10*s.* 6*d.*

Brown.—SANSKRIT PROSODY AND NUMERICAL SYMBOLS EXPLAINED. By CHARLES PHILIP BROWN, Author of the Telugu Dictionary, Grammar, etc., Professor of Telugu in the University of London. Demy 8vo. pp. 64, cloth. 3*s.* 6*d.*

Buddhaghosha's Parables: translated from Burmese by Captain H. T. ROGERS, R.E. With an Introduction containing Buddha's Dhammapadam, or, Path of Virtue; translated from Pali by F. MAX MÜLLER. 8vo. pp. 378, cloth. 12*s.* 6*d.*

Burgess.—SURYA-SIDDHANTA (Translation of the): A Text-book of Hindu Astronomy, with Notes and an Appendix, containing additional Notes and Tables, Calculations of Eclipses, a Stellar Map, and Indexes. By Rev. EBENEZER BURGESS, formerly Missionary of the American Board of Commissioners of Foreign Missions in India; assisted by the Committee of Publication of the American Oriental Society. 8vo. pp. iv. and 354, boards. 15*s.*

Burnell.—CATALOGUE OF A COLLECTION OF SANSKRIT MANUSCRIPTS. By A. C. BURNELL, M.R.A.S., Madras Civil Service. PART 1. *Vedic Manuscripts.* Fcap. 8vo. pp. 64, sewed. 1870. 2*s.*

Byington.—GRAMMAR OF THE CHOCTAW LANGUAGE. By the Rev. CYRUS BYINGTON. Edited from the Original MSS. in the Library of the American Philosophical Society, by D. G. BRINTON, A.M., M.D., Member of the American Philosophical Society, the Pennsylvania Historical Society, Corresponding Member of the American Ethnological Society, etc. 8vo. sewed, pp. 56. 12*s.*

Calcutta Review.—THE CALCUTTA REVIEW. Published Quarterly. Price 8*s.* 6*d.*

Callaway.—Izinganekwane, Nensumansumane, Nezindaba, Zabantu (Nursery Tales, Traditions, and Histories of the Zulus). In their own words, with a Translation into English, and Notes. By the Rev. Henry Callaway, M.D. Volume I., 8vo. pp. xiv. and 378, cloth. Natal, 1866 and 1867. 16*s*.

Callaway. — The Religious System of the Amazulu.

Part I.—Unkulunkulu; or, the Tradition of Creation as existing among the Amazulu and other Tribes of South Africa, in their own words, with a translation into English, and Notes. By the Rev. Canon Callaway, M.D. 8vo. pp. 128, sewed. 1868. 4s.

Part II.—Amatongo; or, Ancestor Worship, as existing among the Amazulu, in their own words, with a translation into English, and Notes. By the Rev. Canon Callaway, M.D. 1869. 8vo. pp. 127, sewed. 1869. 4*s*.

Part III.—Izinyanga Zokubula; or, Divination, as existing among the Amazulu, in their own words. With a Translation into English, and Notes. By the Rev. Canon Callaway, M.D. 8vo. pp. 150, sewed. 1870. 4*s*.

Part IV.—On Medical Magic and Witchcraft. [*In preparation.*

Calligaris.—Le Compagnon de Tous, ou Dictionnaire Polyglotte. Par le Colonel Louis Calligaris, Grand Officier, etc. (French—Latin—Italian—Spanish—Portuguese—German—English—Modern Greek—Arabic—Turkish.) 2 vols. 4to., pp. 1157 and 746. Turin. £4 4s.

Canones Lexicographici; or, Rules to be observed in Editing the New English Dictionary of the Philological Society, prepared by a Committee of the Society. 8vo., pp. 12, sewed. 6*d*.

Carpenter.—The Last Days in England of the Rajah Rammohun Roy. By Mary Carpenter, of Bristol. With Five Illustrations. 8vo. pp. 272, cloth. 7*s*. 6*d*.

Carr.—ఆంధ్రలోకోక్తిచంద్రిక. A Collection of Telugu Proverbs, Translated, Illustrated, and Explained; together with some Sanscrit Proverbs printed in the Devnâgarî and Telugu Characters. By Captain M. W. Carr, Madras Staff Corps. One Vol. and Supplemnt, royal 8vo. pp. 488 and 148. 31*s*. 6*d*

Catlin.—O-Kee-Pa. A Religious Ceremony of the Mandans. By George Catlin. With 13 Coloured Illustrations. 4to. pp. 60, bound in cloth, gilt edges. 14*s*.

Chalmers.—The Origin of the Chinese; an Attempt to Trace the connection of the Chinese with Western Nations in their Religion, Superstitions, Arts, Language, and Traditions. By John Chalmers, A.M. Foolscap 8vo. cloth, pp. 78. 2*s*. 6*d*.

Chalmers.—The Speculations on Metaphysics, Polity, and Morality of "The Old Philosopher" Lau Tsze. Translated from the Chinese, with an Introduction by John Chalmers, M.A. Fcap. 8vo. cloth, xx. and 62. 4*s*. 6*d*.

Chalmers.—An English and Cantonese Pocket-Dictionary, for the use of those who wish to learn the spoken language of Canton Province. By John Chalmers, M.A. Third edition. Crown 8vo., pp. iv. and 146. Hong Kong, 1871. 15*s*.

Charnock.—Ludus Patronymicus; or, the Etymology of Curious Surnames. By Richard Stephen Charnock, Ph.D., F.S.A., F.R.G.S. Crown 8vo., pp. 182, cloth. 7*s*. 6*d*.

Charnock.—Verba Nominalia; or Words derived from Proper Names. By Richard Stephen Charnock, Ph. Dr. F.S.A., etc. 8vo. pp. 326, cloth. 14*s*.

Charnock.—The Peoples of Transylvania. Founded on a Paper read before The Anthropological Society of London, on the 4th of May, 1869. By Richard Stephen Charnock, Ph.D., F.S.A., F.R.G.S. Demy 8vo. pp. 36, sewed. 1870. 2*s*. 6*d*.

Chaucer Society's Publications. Subscription, two guineas per annum.

1868. *First Series.*

CANTERBURY TALES. Part I.

I. The Prologue and Knight's Tale, in 6 parallel Texts (from the 6 MSS. named below), together with Tables, showing the Groups of the Tales, and their varying order in 38 MSS. of the Tales, and in the old printed editions, and also Specimens from several MSS. of the "Moveable Prologues" of the Canterbury Tales,—The Shipman's Prologue, and Franklin's Prologue,—when moved from their right places, and of the substitutes for them.

II.	The Prologue and Knight's Tale from the	Ellesmere MS.	
III.	,, ,, ,, ,, ,, ,, ,,	Hengwrt ,,	154.
IV.	,, ,, ,, ,, ,, ,, ,,	Cambridge ,,	Gg. 4. 27.
V.	,, ,, ,, ,, ,, ,, ,,	Corpus ,,	Oxford.
VI.	,, ,, ,, ,, ,, ,, ,,	Petworth ,,	
VII.	,, ,, ,, ,, ,, ,, ,,	Lansdowne ,,	851.

Nos. II. to VII. are separate Texts of the 6-Text edition of the Canterbury Tales, Part I.

1868. *Second Series.*

ON EARLY ENGLISH PRONUNCIATION, with especial reference to Shakspere and Chaucer, containing an investigation of the Correspondence of Writing with Speech in England, from the Anglo-Saxon period to the present day, preceded by a systematic notation of all spoken sounds, by means of the ordinary printing types. Including a re-arrangement of Prof. F. J. Child's Memoirs on the Language of Chaucer and Gower, and Reprints of the Rare Tracts by Salesbury on English, 1547, and Welsh, 1567, and by Barcley on French, 1521. By ALEXANDER J. ELLIS, F.R.S., etc., etc. Part I. On the Pronunciation of the xivth, xvith, xviith, and xviiith centuries.

ESSAYS ON CHAUCER; His Words and Works. Part I. 1. Ebert's Review of Sandras's *E'tude sur Chaucer, considére comme Imitateur des Trouvères,* translated by J. W. Van Rees Hoets, M.A., Trinity Hall, Cambridge, and revised by the Author.—II. A Thirteenth Century Latin Treatise on the *Chilindre:* "For by my *chilindre* it is prime of day" (*Shipmannes Tale*).. Edited, with a Translation, by Mr. EDMUND BROCK, and illustrated by a Woodcut of the Instrument from the Ashmole MS. 1522.

A TEMPORARY PREFACE to the Six-Text Edition of Chaucer's Canterbury Tales. Part I. Attempting to show the true order of the Tales, and the Days and Stages of the Pilgrimage, etc., etc. By F. J. FURNIVALL, Esq., M.A., Trinity Hall, Cambridge.

1869. *First Series.*

VIII.	The Miller's, Reeve's, Cook's, and Gamelyn's Tales :	Ellesmere MS.
IX.	,, ,, ,, ,, ,, ,, ,,	Hengwrt ,,
X.	,, ,, ,, ,, ,, ,, ,,	Cambridge ,,
XI.	,, ,, ,, ,, ,, ,, ,,	Corpus ,,
XII.	,, ,, ,, ,, ,, ,, ,,	Petworth ,,
XIII.	,, ,, ,, ,, ,, ,, ,,	Lansdowne ,,

These are separate issues of the 6-Text Chaucer's Canterbury Tales, Part II.

1869. *Second Series.*

ENGLISH PRONUNCIATION, with especial reference to Shakspere and Chaucer. By ALEXANDER J. ELLIS, F.R.S. Part II.

1870. *First Series.*

XIV. CANTERBURY TALES. Part II. The Miller's, Reeve's, and Cook's Tales, with an Appendix of the Spurious Tale of Gamelyn, in Six parallel Texts.

Chaucer Society's Publications—*continued.*

1870. *Second Series.*

ON EARLY ENGLISH PRONUNCIATION, with especial reference to Shakspere and Chaucer. By A. J. ELLIS, F.R.S., F.S.A. Part III. Illustrations on the Pronunciation of xivth and xvith Centuries. Chaucer, Gower, Wycliffe, Spenser, Shakespere, Salesbury, Barcley, Hart, Bullokar, Gill. Pronouncing Vocabulary.

1871. *First Series.*

XV. CANTERBURY TALES. Part III. In Six Parallel Texts. The Man of Law's Tale.—The Shipman's Tale.—The Prioress's Tale.—The Tale of Sir Thopas.

XVI. The Man of Law's Tale, &c., &c.: Ellesmere MS.
XVII. „ „ „ „ Cambridge „
XVIII. „ „ „ „ Corpus „
XIX. „ „ „ „ Petworth „
XX. „ „ „ „ Lansdowne „

Childers.—KHUDDAKA PATHA. A Páli Text, with a Translation and Notes. By R. C. CHILDERS, late of the Ceylon Civil Service. 8vo. pp. 32, stitched. 1*s.* 6*d.*

Childers.—A PÁLI-ENGLISH DICTIONARY, with Sanskrit Equivalents, and with numerous Quotations, Extracts, and References. Compiled by R. C. CHILDERS, late of the Ceylon Civil Service. [*In preparation.*

Childers.—A PÁLI GRAMMAR FOR BEGINNERS. By ROBERT C. CHILDERS. In 1 vol. 8vo. cloth. [*In preparation.*

Childers.—NOTES ON DHAMMAPADA, with special reference to the question of Nirvâna. By R. C. CHILDERS, late of the Ceylon Civil Service. 8vo. pp. 12, sewed. Price 1*s.*

Childers.—ON THE ORIGIN OF THE BUDDHIST ARTHAKATHÁS. By the Mudliar L. COMRILLA VIJASINHA, Government Interpreter to the Ratnapura Court, Ceylon. With an Introduction by R. C. CHILDERS, late of the Ceylon Civil Service. 8vo. sewed. 1871. 1*s.*

Clarke.—TEN GREAT RELIGIONS: an Essay in Comparative Theology. By JAMES FREEMAN CLARKE. 8vo. cloth, pp. x. and 528. 1871. 14*s.*

Colebrooke.—THE LIFE AND MISCELLANEOUS ESSAYS OF HENRY THOMAS COLEBROOKE. The Biography by his Son, Sir T. E. COLEBROOKE, Bart., M.P., The Essays edited by Professor Cowell. In 3 vols. [*In the press.*

Colenso.—FIRST STEPS IN ZULU-KAFIR: An Abridgement of the Elementary Grammar of the Zulu-Kafir Language. By the Right Rev. JOHN W. COLENSO, Bishop of Natal. 8vo. pp. 86, cloth. Ekukanyeni, 1859. 4*s.* 6*d.*

Colenso.—ZULU-ENGLISH DICTIONARY. By the Right Rev. JOHN W. COLENSO, Bishop of Natal. 8vo. pp. viii. and 552, sewed. Pietermaritzburg, 1861. £1 1*s.*

Colenso.—FIRST ZULU-KAFIR READING BOOK, two parts in one. By the Right Rev. JOHN W. COLENSO, Bishop of Natal. 16mo. pp. 44, sewed. Natal. 1*s.*

Colenso.—SECOND ZULU-KAFIR READING BOOK. By the same. 16mo. pp. 108, sewed. Natal. 3*s.*

Colenso.—FOURTH ZULU-KAFIR READING BOOK. By the same. 8vo. pp. 160, cloth. Natal, 1859. 7*s.*

Colenso.—Three Native Accounts of the Visits of the Bishop of Natal in September and October, 1859, to Upmande, King of the Zulus; with Explanatory Notes and a Literal Translation, and a Glossary of all the Zulu Words employed in the same: designed for the use of Students of the Zulu Language. By the Right Rev. JOHN W. COLENSO, Bishop of Natal. 16mo. pp. 160, stiff cover. Natal, Maritzburg, 1860. 4*s.* 6*d.*

Coleridge.—A GLOSSARIAL INDEX to the Printed English Literature of the Thirteenth Century. By HERBERT COLERIDGE, Esq. 8vo. cloth. pp. 104, 2*s.* 6*d.*

Colleccao de Vocabulos e Frases usados na Provincia de S. Pedro, do Rio Grande do Sul, no Brasil. 12mo. pp. 32, sewed. 1*s.*

Contopoulos.—A Lexicon of Modern Greek-English and English Modern Greek. By N. Contopoulos.

Part I. Modern Greek-English. 8vo. cloth, pp. 460. 12*s.*
Part II. English-Modern Greek. 8vo. cloth, pp. 582. 15*s.*

Cunningham.—The Ancient Geography of India. I. The Buddhist Period, including the Campaigns of Alexander, and the Travels of Hwen-Thsang. By Alexander Cunningham, Major-General, Royal Engineers (Bengal Retired). With thirteen Maps. 8vo. pp. xx. 590, cloth. 1870. 28*s.*

Cunningham.—An Essay on the Arian Order of Architecture, as exhibited in the Temples of Kashmere. By Captain (now Major-General) Alexander Cunningham. 8vo. pp. 86, cloth. With seventeen large folding Plates. 18*s.*

Cunningham.—The Bhilsa Topes; or, Buddhist Monuments of Central India: comprising a brief Historical Sketch of the Rise, Progress, and Decline of Buddhism; with an Account of the Opening and Examination of the various Groups of Topes around Bhilsa. By Brev.-Major Alexander Cunningham, Bengal Engineers. Illustrated with thirty-three Plates. 8vo. pp. xxxvi. 370, cloth. 1854. 21*s.*

D'Alwis.—A Descriptive Catalogue of Sanskrit, Pali, and Sinhalese Literary Works of Ceylon. By James D'Alwis, M.R.A.S., Advocate of the Supreme Court, &c., &c. In Three Volumes. Vol. I., pp. xxxii. and 244, sewed. 1870. 8*s.* 6*d.* [*Vols. II. and III. in preparation.*

De Gubernatis.—Mythical Zoology; or, the Legends of Animals. By Angelo de Gubernatis, Professor of Sanskrit and Comparative Literature at Florence. [*In the press.*

Delepierre.—Revue Analytique des Ouvrages Écrits en Centons, depuis les Temps Anciens, jusqu'au xixième Siècle. Par un Bibliophile Belge. Small 4to. pp. 508, stiff covers. 1868. 30*s.*

Delepierre.—Essai Historique et Bibliographique sur les Rébus. Par Octave Delepierre. 8vo. pp. 24, sewed. With 15 pages of Woodcuts. 1870. 3*s.* 6*d.*

Dennys.—China and Japan. A complete Guide to the Open Ports of those countries, together with Pekin, Yeddo, Hong Kong, and Macao; forming a Guide Book and Vade Mecum for Travellers, Merchants, and Residents in general; with 56 Maps and Plans. By Wm. Frederick Mayers, F.R.G.S. H.M.'s Consular Service; N. B. Dennys, late H.M.'s Consular Service; and Charles King, Lieut. Royal Marine Artillery. Edited by N. B. Dennys. In one volume. 8vo. pp. 600, cloth. £2 2*s.*

Döhne.—A Zulu-Kafir Dictionary, etymologically explained, with copious illustrations and examples, preceded by an introduction on the Zulu-Kafir Language. By the Rev. J. L. Döhne. Royal 8vo. pp. xlii. and 418, sewed. Cape Town, 1857. 21*s.*

Döhne.—The Four Gospels in Zulu. By the Rev. J. L. Döhne, Missionary to the American Board, C.F.M. 8vo. pp. 208, cloth. Pietermaritzburg, 1866. 5*s.*

Doolittle.—An English and Chinese Dictionary. By the Rev. Justus Doolittle, China. [*In the Press.*

Dowson.—A Grammar of the Hindustani Language. By John Dowson, M.R.A.S., Staff College, Sandhurst. Cr. 8vo. [*In the press.*

Early English Text Society's Publications. Subscription, one guinea per annum.

1. Early English Alliterative Poems. In the West-Midland Dialect of the Fourteenth Century. Edited by R. Morris, Esq., from an unique Cottonian MS. 16*s.*
2. Arthur (about 1440 A.D.). Edited by F. J. Furnivall, Esq., from the Marquis of Bath's unique MS. 4*s.*
3. Ane Compendious and Breue Tractate concernyng ye Office and Dewtie of Kyngis, etc. By William Lauder. (1556 A.D.) Edited by F. Hall, Esq., D.C.L. 4*s.*
4. Sir Gawayne and the Green Knight (about 1320-30 A.D.). Edited by R. Morris, Esq., from an unique Cottonian MS. 10*s.*
5. Of the Orthographie and Congruitie of the Britan Tongue; a treates, noe shorter than necessarie, for the Schooles, be Alexander Hume. Edited for the first time from the unique MS. in the British Museum (about 1617 A.D.), by Henry B. Wheatley, Esq. 4*s.*
6. Lancelot of the Laik. Edited from the unique MS. in the Cambridge University Library (ab. 1500), by the Rev. Walter W. Skeat, M.A. 8*s.*
7. The Story of Genesis and Exodus, an Early English Song, of about 1250 A.D. Edited for the first time from the unique MS. in the Library of Corpus Christi College, Cambridge, by R. Morris, Esq. 8*s.*
8. Morte Arthure; the Alliterative Version. Edited from Robert Thornton's unique MS. (about 1440 A.D.) at Lincoln, by the Rev. George Perry, M.A., Prebendary of Lincoln. 7*s.*
9. Animadversions uppon the Annotacions and Corrections of some Imperfections of Impressiones of Chaucer's Workes, reprinted in 1598; by Francis Thynne. Edited from the unique MS. in the Bridgewater Library. By G. H. Kingsley, Esq., M.D. 4*s.*
10. Merlin, or the Early History of King Arthur. Edited for the first time from the unique MS. in the Cambridge University Library (about 1450 A.D.), by Henry B. Wheatley, Esq. Part I. 2*s.* 6*d.*
11. The Monarche, and other Poems of Sir David Lyndesay. Edited from the first edition by Johne Skott, in 1552, by Fitzedward Hall, Esq., D.C.L. Part I. 3*s.*
12. The Wright's Chaste Wife, a Merry Tale, by Adam of Cobsam (about 1462 A.D.), from the unique Lambeth MS. 306. Edited for the first time by F. J. Furnivall, Esq., M.A. 1*s.*
13. Seinte Marherete, þe Meiden ant Martyr. Three Texts of ab. 1200, 1310, 1330 A.D. First edited in 1862, by the Rev. Oswald Cockayne, M.A., and now re-issued. 2*s.*
14. Kyng Horn, with fragments of Floriz and Blauncheflur, and the Assumption of the Blessed Virgin. Edited from the MSS. in the Library of the University of Cambridge and the British Museum, by the Rev. J. Rawson Lumby. 3*s.* 6*d.*
15. Political, Religious, and Love Poems, from the Lambeth MS. No. 306, and other sources. Edited by F. J. Furnivall, Esq., M.A. 7*s.* 6*d.*
16. A Tretice in English breuely drawe out of þ book of Quintis essencijs in Latyn, þ Hermys þ prophete and king of Egipt after þ flood of Noe, fader of Philosophris, hadde by reuelacioun of an aungil of God to him sente. Edited from the Sloane MS. 73, by F. J. Furnivall, Esq., M.A. 1*s.*
17. Parallel Extracts from 29 Manuscripts of Piers Plowman, with Comments, and a Proposal for the Society's Three-text edition of this Poem. By the Rev. W. Skeat, M.A. 1*s.*
18. Hali Meidenhead, about 1200 A.D. Edited for the first time from the MS. (with a translation) by the Rev. Oswald Cockayne, M.A. 1*s.*

Early English Text Society's Publications—*continued.*

19. THE MONARCHE, and other Poems of Sir David Lyndesay. Part II., the Complaynt of the King's Papingo, and other minor Poems. Edited from the First Edition by F. HALL, Esq., D.C.L. 3*s.* 6*d.*

20. SOME TREATISES BY RICHARD ROLLE DE HAMPOLE. Edited from Robert of Thornton's MS. (ab. 1440 A.D.), by Rev. GEORGE G. PERRY, M.A. 1*s.*

21. MERLIN, OR THE EARLY HISTORY OF KING ARTHUR. Part II. Edited by HENRY B. WHEATLEY, Esq. 4*s.*

22. THE ROMANS OF PARTENAY, OR LUSIGNEN. Edited for the first time from the unique MS. in the Library of Trinity College, Cambridge, by the Rev. W. W. SKEAT, M.A. 6*s.*

23. DAN MICHEL'S AYENBITE OF INWYT, or Remorse of Conscience, in the Kentish dialect, 1340 A.D. Edited from the unique MS. in the British Museum, by RICHARD MORRIS, Esq. 10*s.* 6*d.*

24. HYMNS OF THE VIRGIN AND CHRIST; THE PARLIAMENT OF DEVILS, and Other Religious Poems. Edited from the Lambeth MS. 853, by F. J. FURNIVALL, M.A. 3*s.*

25. THE STACIONS OF ROME, and the Pilgrim's Sea-Voyage and Sea-Sickness, with Clene Maydenhod. Edited from the Vernon and Porkington MSS., etc., by F. J. FURNIVALL, Esq., M.A. 1*s.*

26. RELIGIOUS PIECES IN PROSE AND VERSE. Containing Dan Jon Gaytrigg's Sermon; The Abbaye of S. Spirit; Sayne Jon, and other pieces in the Northern Dialect. Edited from Robert of Thorntone's MS. (ab. 1460 A.D.), by the Rev. G. PERRY, M.A. 2*s.*

27. MANIPULUS VOCABULORUM: a Rhyming Dictionary of the English Language, by PETER LEVINS (1570). Edited, with an Alphabetical Index, by HENRY B. WHEATLEY. 12*s.*

28. THE VISION OF WILLIAM CONCERNING PIERS PLOWMAN, together with Vita de Dowel, Dobet et Dobest. 1362 A.D., by WILLIAM LANGLAND. The earliest or Vernon Text; Text A. Edited from the Vernon MS., with full Collations, by Rev. W. W. SKEAT, M.A. 7*s.*

29. OLD ENGLISH HOMILIES AND HOMILETIC TREATISES. (Sawles Warde and the Wohunge of Ure Lauerd: Ureisuns of Ure Louerd and of Ure Lefdi, etc.) of the Twelfth and Thirteenth Centuries. Edited from MSS. in the British Museum, Lambeth, and Bodleian Libraries; with Introduction, Translation, and Notes. By RICHARD MORRIS. *First Series.* Part I. 7*s.*

30. PIERS, THE PLOUGHMAN'S CREDE (about 1394). Edited from the MSS. by the Rev. W. W. SKEAT, M.A. 2*s.*

31. INSTRUCTIONS FOR PARISH PRIESTS. By JOHN MYRC. Edited from Cotton MS. Claudius A. II., by EDWARD PEACOCK, Esq., F.S.A., etc., etc. 4*s.*

32. THE BABEES BOOK, Aristotle's A B C, Urbanitatis, Stans Puer ad Mensam, The Lytille Childrenes Lytil Boke. THE BOKES OF NURTURE of Hugh Rhodes and John Russell, Wynkyn de Worde's Boke of Kervynge, The Booke of Demeanor, The Boke of Curtasye, Seager's Schoole of Vertue, etc., etc. With some French and Latin Poems on like subjects, and some Forewords on Education in Early England. Edited by F. J. FURNIVALL, M.A., Trin. Hall, Cambridge. 15*s.*

33. THE BOOK OF THE KNIGHT DE LA TOUR LANDRY, 1372. A Father's Book for his Daughters, Edited from the Harleian MS. 1764, by THOMAS WRIGHT, Esq., M.A., and Mr. WILLIAM ROSSITER. 8*s.*

34. OLD ENGLISH HOMILIES AND HOMILETIC TREATISES. (Sawles Warde, and the Wohunge of Ure Lauerd: Ureisuns of Ure Louerd and of Ure Lefdi, etc.) of the Twelfth and Thirteenth Centuries. Edited from MSS. in the British Museum, Lambeth, and Bodleian Libraries; with Introduction, Translation, and Notes, by RICHARD MORRIS. *First Series.* Part 2. 8*s.*

Early English English Text Society's Publications—*continued.*

35. Sir David Lyndesay's Works. Part 3. The Historie of ane Nobil and Wailzeand Sqvyer, William Meldrum, umqvhyle Laird of Cleische and Bynnis, compylit be Sir Dauid Lyndesay of the Mont *alias* Lyoun King of Armes. With the Testament of the said Williame Meldrum, Squyer, compylit alswa be Sir Dauid Lyndesay, etc. Edited by F. Hall, D.C.L. 2*s.*

36. Merlin, or the Early History of King Arthur. A Prose Romance (about 1450–1460 A.D.), edited from the unique MS. in the University Library, Cambridge, by Henry B. Wheatley. With an Essay on Arthurian Localities, by J. S. Stuart Glennie, Esq. Part III. 1869. 12*s.*

37. Sir David Lyndesay's Works. Part IV. Ane Satyre of the thrie estaits, in commendation of vertew and vitvperation of vyce. Maid be Sir David Lindesay, of the Mont, *alias* Lyon King of Armes. At Edinbvrgh. Printed be Robert Charteris, 1602. Cvm privilegio regis. Edited by F. Hall, Esq., D.C.L. 4*s.*

38. The Vision of William concerning Piers the Plowman, together with Vita de Dowel, Dobet, et Dobest, Secundum Wit et Resoun, by William Langland (1377 A.D.). The "Crowley" Text; or Text B. Edited from MS. Laud Misc. 581, collated with MS. Rawl. Poet. 38, MS. B. 15. 17. in the Library of Trinity College, Cambridge, MS. Dd. 1. 17. in the Cambridge University Library, the MS. in Oriel College, Oxford, MS. Bodley 814, etc. By the Rev. Walter W. Skeat, M.A., late Fellow of Christ's College, Cambridge. 10*s.* 6*d.*

39. The "Gest Hystoriale" of the Destruction of Troy. An Alliterative Romance, translated from Guido De Colonna's "Hystoria Troiana." Now first edited from the unique MS. in the Hunterian Museum, University of Glasgow, by the Rev. Geo. A. Panton and David Donaldson. Part I. 10*s.* 6*d.*

40. English Gilds. The Original Ordinances of more than One Hundred Early English Gilds: Together with the olde usages of the cite of Wynchestre; The Ordinances of Worcester; The Office of the Mayor of Bristol; and the Customary of the Manor of Tettenhall-Regis. From Original MSS. of the Fourteenth and Fifteenth Centuries. Edited with Notes by the late Toulmin Smith, Esq., F.R.S. of Northern Antiquaries (Copenhagen). With an Introduction and Glossary, etc., by his daughter, Lucy Toulmin Smith. And a Preliminary Essay, in Five Parts, On the History and Development of Gilds, by Lujo Brentano, Doctor Juris Utriusque et Philosophiæ. 21*s.*

41. The Minor Poems of William Lauder, Playwright, Poet, and Minister of the Word of God (mainly on the State of Scotland in and about 1568 A.D., that year of Famine and Plague). Edited from the Unique Originals belonging to S. Christie-Miller, Esq., of Britwell, by F. J. Furnivall, M.A., Trin. Hall, Camb. 3*s.*

42. Bernardus de Cura rei Famuliaris, with some Early Scotch Prophecies, etc. From a MS., KK 1. 5, in the Cambridge University Library. Edited by J. Rawson Lumby, M.A., late Fellow of Magdalen College, Cambridge. 2*s.*

43. Ratis Raving, and other Moral and Religious Pieces, in Prose and Verse. Edited from the Cambridge University Library MS. KK 1. 5, by J. Rawson Lumby, M.A., late Fellow of Magdalen College, Cambridge. 3*s.*

44. Joseph of Arimathie: otherwise called the Romance of the Seint Graal, or Holy Grail: an alliterative poem, written about A.D. 1350, and now first printed from the unique copy in the Vernon MS. at Oxford. With an appendix, containing "The Lyfe of Joseph of Armathy," reprinted from the black-letter copy of Wynkyn de Worde; "De sancto Joseph ab Arimathia," first printed by Pynson, A.D. 1516; and "The Lyfe of Joseph of Arimathia," first printed by Pynson, A.D. 1520. Edited, with Notes and Glossarial Indices, by the Rev. Walter W. Skeat, M.A. 5*s.*

Early English Text Society's Publications—*continued.*

45. KING ALFRED'S WEST-SAXON VERSION OF GREGORY'S PASTORAL CARE. With an English translation, the Latin Text, Notes, and an Introduction Edited by HENRY SWEET, Esq., of Balliol College, Oxford. Part I. *10s.*

46. LEGENDS OF THE HOLY ROOD; SYMBOLS OF THE PASSION AND CROSS-POEMS. In Old English of the Eleventh, Fourteenth, and Fifteenth Centuries. Edited from MSS. in the British Museum and Bodleian Libraries; with Introduction, Translations, and Glossarial Index. By RICHARD MORRIS, LL.D. *10s.*

47. SIR DAVID LYNDESAY'S WORKS. PART V. The Minor Poems of Lyndesay. Edited by J. A. H. MURRAY, Esq. *3s.*

48. THE TIMES' WHISTLE: or, A Newe Daunce of Seven Satires, and other Poems: Compiled by R. C., Gent. Now first Edited from MS. Y. 8. 3. in the Library of Canterbury Cathedral; with Introduction, Notes, and Glossary, by J. M. COWPER. *6s.*

Extra Series. Subscriptions—Small paper, one guinea; large paper two guineas, per annum.

1. THE ROMANCE OF WILLIAM OF PALERNE (otherwise known as the Romance of William and the Werwolf). Translated from the French at the command of Sir Humphrey de Bohun, about A.D. 1350, to which is added a fragment of the Alliterative Romance of Alisaunder, translated from the Latin by the same author, about A.D. 1340; the former re-edited from the unique MS. in the Library of King's College, Cambridge, the latter now first edited from the unique MS. in the Bodleian Library, Oxford. By the Rev. WALTER W. SKEAT, M.A. 8vo. sewed, pp. xliv. and 328. *£1 6s.*

2. ON EARLY ENGLISH PRONUNCIATION, with especial reference to Shakspere and Chaucer; containing an investigation of the Correspondence of Writing with Speech in England, from the Anglo-Saxon period to the present day, preceded by a systematic Notation of all Spoken Sounds by means of the ordinary Printing Types; including a re-arrangement of Prof. F. J. Child's Memoirs on the Language of Chaucer and Gower, and reprints of the rare Tracts by Salesbury on English, 1547, and Welsh, 1567, and by Barcley on French, 1521. By ALEXANDER J. ELLIS, F.R.S. Part I. On the Pronunciation of the XIVth, XVIth, XVIIth, and XVIIIth centuries. 8vo. sewed, pp. viii. and 416. *10s.*

3. CAXTON'S BOOK OF CURTESYE, printed at Westminster about 1477–8, A.D., and now reprinted, with two MS. copies of the same treatise, from the Oriel MS. 79, and the Balliol MS. 354. Edited by FREDERICK J. FURNIVALL, M.A. 8vo. sewed, pp. xli. and 58. *5s.*

4. THE LAY OF HAVELOK THE DANE; composed in the reign of Edward I., about A.D. 1280. Formerly edited by Sir F. MADDEN for the Roxburghe Club, and now re-edited from the unique MS. Laud Misc. 108, in the Bodleian Library, Oxford, by the Rev. WALTER W. SKEAT, M.A. 8vo. sewed, pp. lv. and 160. *10s.*

5. CHAUCER'S TRANSLATION OF BOETHIUS'S "DE CONSOLATIONE PHILOSOPHIE." Edited from the Additional MS. 10,340 in the British Museum. Collated with the Cambridge Univ. Libr. MS. Ii. 3. 21. By RICHARD MORRIS. 8vo. *12s.*

6 THE ROMANCE OF THE CHEVELERE ASSIGNE. Re-edited from the unique manuscript in the British Museum, with a Preface, Notes, and Glossarial Index, by HENRY H. GIBBS, Esq., M.A. 8vo. sewed, pp. xviii. and 38. *3s.*

Early English Text Society's Publications—*continued.*

7. On Early English Pronunciation, with especial reference to Shakspere and Chaucer. By Alexander J. Ellis, F.R.S., etc., etc. Part II. On the Pronunciation of the xiii th and previous centuries, of Anglo-Saxon, Icelandic, Old Norse and Gothic, with Chronological Tables of the Value of Letters and Expression of Sounds in English Writing. 10*s.*

8. Queene Elizabethes Achademy, by Sir Humphrey Gilbert. A Booke of Precedence, The Ordering of a Funerall, etc. Varying Versions of the Good Wife, The Wise Man, etc., Maxims, Lydgate's Order of Fools, A Poem on Heraldry, Occleve on Lords' Men, etc., Edited by F. J. Furnivall, M.A., Trin. Hall, Camb. With Essays on Early Italian and German Books of Courtesy, by W. M. Rossetti, Esq., and E. Oswald, Esq. 8vo. 13*s.*

9. The Fraternitye of Vacabondes, by John Awdeley (licensed in 1560-1, imprinted then, and in 1565), from the edition of 1575 in the Bodleian Library. A Caueat or Warening for Commen Cursetors vulgarely called Vagabones, by Thomas Harman, Esquiere. From the 3rd edition of 1567, belonging to Henry Huth, Esq., collated with the 2nd edition of 1567, in the Bodleian Library, Oxford, and with the reprint of the 4th edition of 1573. A Sermon in Praise of Thieves and Thievery, by Parson Haben or Hyberdyne, from the Lansdowne MS. 98, and Cotton Vesp. A. 25. Those parts of the Groundworke of Conny-catching (ed. 1592), that differ from *Harman's Caueat.* Edited by Edward Viles & F. J. Furnivall. 8vo. 7*s.* 6*d.*

10. The Fyrst Boke of the Introduction of Knowledge, made by Andrew Borde, of Physycke Doctor. A Compendyous Regyment of a Dyetary of Helth made in Mountpyllier, compiled by Andrewe Boorde, of Physycke Doctor. Barnes in the Defence of the Berde: a treatyse made, answerynge the treatyse of Doctor Borde upon Berdes. Edited, with a life of Andrew Boorde, and large extracts from his Breuyary, by F. J. Furnivall, M.A., Trinity Hall, Camb. 8vo. 18*s.*

11. The Bruce; or, the Book of the most excellent and noble Prince, Robert de Broyss. King of Scots: compiled by Master John Barbour, Archdeacon of Aberdeen. A.D. 1375. Edited from MS. G 23 in the Library of St. John's College, Cambridge, written A.D. 1487; collated with the MS. in the Advocates' Library at Edinburgh, written A.D. 1489, and with Hart's Edition, printed A.D. 1616; with a Preface, Notes, and Glossarial Index, by the Rev. Walter W. Skeat, M.A. Part I. 8vo. 12*s.*

12. England in the Reign of King Henry the Eighth. A Dialogue between Cardinal Pole and Thomas Lupset, Lecturer in Rhetoric at Oxford. By Thom s Starkey, Chaplain to the King. Edited, with Preface, Notes, and Glossary, by J. M. Cowper. And with an Introduction containing the Life and Letters of Thomas Starkey, by the Rev. J. S. Brewer, M.A. Part II. 12*s.*

(*Part I., Starkey's Life and Letters, is in preparation.*

13. A Supplicacyon for the Beggars. Written about the year 1529, by Simon Fish. Now re-edited by Frederick J. Furnivall. With a Supplycacion to our moste Soueraigne Lorde Kynge Henry the Eyght (1544 A.D.), A Supplication of the Poore Commons (1546 A.D.), The Decaye of England by the great multitude of Shepe (1550–3 A.D.). Edited by J. Meadows Cowper. 6*s.*

14. On Early English Pronunciation, with especial reference to Shakspere and Chaucer. By A. J. Ellis, F.R.S., F.S.A. Part III. Illustrations of the Pronunciation of the xivth and xvith Centuries. Chaucer, Gower, Wycliffe, Spenser, Shakspere, Salesbury, Barcley, Hart, Bullokar, Gill. Pronouncing Vocabulary. 10*s.*

Edda Saemundar Hinns Froda—The Edda of Saemund the Learned. From the Old Norse or Icelandic. Part I. with a Mythological Index. 12mo. pp. 152, cloth, 3*s.* 6*d.* Part II. with Index of Persons and Places. By Benjamin Thorpe. 12mo. pp. viii. and 172, cloth. 1866. 4*s.*; or in 1 Vol. complete, 7*s.* 6*d.*

Edkins.—China's Place in Philology. An attempt to show that the Languages of Europe and Asia have a common origin. By the Rev. Joseph Edkins. Crown 8vo., pp. xxiii.—403, cloth. 10*s.* 6*d.*

Edkins.—A Vocabulary of the Shanghai Dialect. By J. Edkins. 8vo. half-calf, pp. vi. and 151. Shanghai, 1869. 21*s.*

Edkins.—A Grammar of Colloquial Chinese, as exhibited in the Shanghai Dialect. By J. Edkins, B.A. Second edition, corrected. 8vo. half-calf, pp. viii. and 225. Shanghai, 1868. 21*s.*

Edkins.—A Grammar of the Chinese Colloquial Language, commonly called the Mandarin Dialect. By Joseph Edkins. Second edition. 8vo. half-calf, pp. viii. and 279. Shanghai, 1864. £1 10*s.*

Eger and Grime; an Early English Romance. Edited from Bishop Percy's Folio Manuscript, about 1650 A.D. By John W. Hales, M.A., Fellow and late Assistant Tutor of Christ's College, Cambridge, and Frederick J. Furnivall, M.A., of Trinity Hall, Cambridge. 1 vol. 4to., pp. 64, (only 100 copies printed), bound in the Roxburghe style. 10*s.* 6*d.*

Eitel.—Handbook for the Student of Chinese Buddhism. By the Rev. E. J. Eitel, of the London Missionary Society. Crown 8vo. pp. viii., 224, cl., 18*s.*

Eitel.—Three Lectures on Buddhism. By Rev. Ernest J. Eitel. Medium 8vo., pp. 42, sewed. 3*s.* 6*d.*

Eitel.—Sketches from Life among the Hakkas of Southern China. By the Rev. E. J. Eitel, Hong-Kong. [*In preparation.*

Elliot.—The History of India, as told by its own Historians. The Muhammadan Period. Edited from the Posthumous Papers of the late Sir H. M. Elliot, K.C.B., East India Company's Bengal Civil Service, by Prof. John Dowson, M.R.A.S., Staff College, Sandhurst.

Vols. I. and II. With a Portrait of Sir H. M. Elliot. 8vo. pp xxxii. and 542, x. and 580, cloth. 18*s.* each.

Vol. III. 8vo. pp. xii. and 627, cloth. 24*s.*

Elliot.—Memoirs on the History, Folklore, and Distribution of the Races of the North Western Provinces of India; being an amplified Edition of the original Supplementary Glossary of Indian Terms. By the late Sir Henry M. Elliot, K.C.B., of the Hon. East India Company's Bengal Civil Service. Edited, revised, and re-arranged, by John Beames, M.R.A.S., Bengal Civil Service; Member of the German Oriental Society, of the Asiatic Societies of Paris and Bengal, and of the Philological Society of London. In 2 vols. demy 8vo., pp. xx., 370, and 396, cloth. With two Lithographic Plates, one full-page coloured Map, and three large coloured folding Maps. 36*s.*

Ellis.—The Asiatic Affinities of the Old Italians. By Robert Ellis, B.D., Fellow of St. John's College, Cambridge, and author of "Ancient Routes between Italy and Gaul." Crown 8vo. pp. iv. 156, cloth. 1870. 5*s.*

English and Welsh Languages.—The Influence of the English and Welsh Languages upon each other, exhibited in the Vocabularies of the two Tongues. Intended to suggest the importance to Philologers, Antiquaries, Ethnographers, and others, of giving due attention to the Celtic Branch of the Indo-Germanic Family of Languages. Square, pp. 30, sewed. 1869. 1*s.*

Etherington.—The Student's Grammar of the Hindí Language. By the Rev. W. Etherington, Missionary, Benares. Crown 8vo. pp. xii. 220. xlviii. cloth. 1870. 10*s.* 6*d.*

Ethnological Society of London (The Journal of the). Edited by Professor Huxley, F.R.S., President of the Society; George Busk, Esq., F.R.S.; Sir John Lubbock, Bart., F.R.S.; Colonel A. Lane Fox, Hon. Sec.; Thomas Wright, Esq., Hon. Sec.; Hyde Clarke, Esq.; Sub-Editor; and Assistant Secretary, J. H. Lamprey, Esq. Published Quarterly.

Vol. I., No. 1. April, 1869. 8vo. pp. 88, sewed. 3*s.*

Contents.—Flint Instruments from Oxfordshire and the Isle of Thanet. (Illustrated.) By Colonel A. Lane Fox.—The Westerly Drifting of Nomads. By H. H. Howorth.—On the Lion Shilling. By Hyde Clarke.—Letter on a Marble Armlet. By H. W. Edwards.—On a Bronze

Spear from Lough Gur, Limerick. (Illustrated.) By Col. A. Lane Fox.—On Chinese Charms. By W. H. Black.—Proto-ethnic Condition of Asia Minor. By Hyde Clarke.—On Stone Implements from the Cape. (Illustrated.) By Sir J. Lubbock.—Cromlechs and Megalithic Structures. By H. M. Westropp.—Remarks on Mr. Westropp's Paper. By Colonel A. Lane Fox.—Stone Implements from San José. By A. Steffens.—On Child-bearing in Australia and New Zealand. By J. Hooker, M.D.—On a Pseudo-cromlech on Mount Alexander, Australia. By Acheson.—The Cave Cannibals of South Africa. By Layland.—Reviews: Wallace's Malay Archipelago (with illustrations); Fryer's Hill Tribes of India (with an illustration); Reliquiæ Aquitanicæ, etc.—Method of Photographic Measurement of the Human Frame (with an illustration). By J. H. Lamprey.—Notes and Queries.

Vol. I., No. 2. July, 1869. 8vo. pp. 117, sewed. 3*s*.

CONTENTS.—Ordinary Meeting, March 9, 1869 (held at the Museum of Practical Geology), Professor Huxley, F.R.S., President, in the Chair. Opening Address of the President.—On the Characteristics of the population of Central and South India (Illustrated). By Sir Walter Elliot.—On the Races of India as traced in existing Tribes and Castes (With a Map). By G. Campbell, Esq.—Remarks by Mr. James Fergusson.—Remarks by Mr. Walter Dendy.—Ordinary Meeting, January 23rd, 1869. Professor Huxley, F.R.S., President, in the Chair. On the Lepchas. By Dr. A. Campbell, late Superintendent of Darjeeling.—On Pre-historic Archæology of India (Illustrated). By Colonel Meadows Taylor, C.S.I., M.R.A.S., M.R.I.A., etc.—Appendix I. Extract from description of the Pandoo Coolies in Malabar. By J. Babington, Esq. (Read before the Literary Society of Bombay, December 20th, 1820. Published in Volume III. of the Society's Transactions).—Appendix II. Extract from a letter from Captain, now Colonel, A. Doria, dated Camp Katangrich, April 12th, 1852.—On some of the Mountain Tribes of the North Western frontier of India. By Major Fosbery, V.C.—On Permanence of type in the Human Race. By Sir William Denison.—Notes and Reviews.—Ethnological Notes and Queries.—Notices of Ethnology.

Vol. I., No. 3. October, 1869. pp. 137, sewed. 3*s*.

CONTENTS.—On the Excavation of a large raised Stone Circle or Barrow, near the Village of Wurreegaon, one mile from the military station of Kamptee, Central Provinces of India (Illustrated). By Major George Godfrey Pearse, Royal Artillery.—Remarks by Dr. Hooker on Dr. Campbell's paper.—North-American Ethnology: Address of the President.—On the Native Races of New Mexico (Illustrated). By Dr. A. W. Bell.—On the Arapahoes, Kiowas, and Comanches. By Morton C. Fisher.—The North-American Indians: a Sketch of some of the hostile Tribes; together with a brief account of General Sheridan's Campaign of 1868 against the Sioux, Cheyenne, Arapahoe, Kiowa, and Comanche Indians. By William Blackmore.—Notes and Reviews: The Ethnological Essays of William Ewart Gladstone. Juventus Mundi, the Gods and Men of the Homeric Age. By the Right Hon. William Ewart Gladstone. (The Review by Hyde Clarke, Esq.)—Notes and Queries.—Classification Committee.

Vol. I., No. 4. January, 1870. 8vo. pp. 98, sewed. 3*s*.

CONTENTS.—On New Zealand and Polynesian Ethnology: On the Social Life of the ancient Inhabitants of New Zealand, and on the national character it was likely to form. By Sir George Grey, K.C.B.—Notes on the Maories of New Zealand and some Melanesians of the south-west Pacific. By the Bishop of Wellington.—Observations on the Inhabitants and Antiquities of Easter Island. By J. L. Palmer.—On the westerly drifting of Nomades from the fifth to the nineteenth century. Part II. The Seljuks, Ghazdevides, etc. By H. H. Howorth, Esq.—Settle Cave Exploration.—Index.—Contents.—Report of the Council.—List of Fellows.

Vol. II., No. 1. April, 1870. 8vo. pp. 96, sewed. 3*s*.

CONTENTS:—On the Proposed Exploration of Stonehenge by a Committee of the British Association. By Col. A. Lane Fox.—On the Chinese Race, their Language, Government, Social Institutions, and Religion. By C. T. Gardner. Appendix I.: On Chinese Mythological and Legendary History. II.: On Chinese Time.—Discussion.—On the Races and Languages of Dardistan. By Dr. G. W. Leitner.—Discussion.—Extract from a Communication by Munphool, Pundit to the Political Department, India Office, on the Relations between Gilgit, Chitral, and Kashmir.—On Quartzite Implements from the Cape of Good Hope. By Sir G. Grey.—Discussion.—Note on a supposed Stone Implement from County Wicklow, Ireland. By F. Atcheson.—Note on the Stature of American Indians of the Chipewyan Tribe. By Major-General Lefroy—Report on the Present State and Condition of Pre-historic Remains in the Channel Islands. By Lieut. S. P. Oliver.—Appendix: The Opening and Restoration of the Cromlech of Le Couperon.—Discussion.—Description and Remarks upon an Ancient *Calvaria* from China, which has been *supposed* to be that of Confucius. By George Busk.—Discussion.—On the Westerly Drifting of Nomades, from the 5th to the 19th Century. Part III. The Comans and Petchenegs. By H. H. Howorth.—Review.—Notes and Queries.—Illustrated.

Vol. II., No. 2. July, 1870. 8vo. pp. 95, sewed. 3*s*.

CONTENTS:—On the Kitai and Kara-Kitai. By Dr. G. Oppert.—Discussion.—Note on the Use of the New Zealand Mere. By Colonel A. Lane Fox.—On Certain Pre-historic Remains discovered in New Zealand, and on the Nature of the Deposits in which they occurred. By Dr. Julius Haast.—Discussion.—On the Origin of the Tasmanians, geologically considered. By James Bonwick.—Discussion.—On a Frontier Line of Ethnology and Geology. By H. H. Howorth.—Notes on the Nicobar Islanders. By G. M. Atkinson.—On the Discovery of Flint and Chert under a Submerged Forest in West Somerset. By W. Boyd Dawkins.—Discussion.—Remarks by Dr. A. Campbell, introductory to the Rev. R. J. Mapleton's Report.—Report on Pre-historic Remains in the Neighbourhood of the Crinan Canal, Argyllshire. By the Rev. R. J. Mapleton.—Discussion.—Supplementary Remarks to a Note on an Ancient Chinese Calva. By George Busk.—On Discoveries in Recent Deposits in Yorkshire. By C. Monkman.—Discussion.—On the Natives of Naga, in Luzon, Philippine Islands.—By Dr. Jagor.—On the Koords. By Major F. Millinger.—On the Westerly Drifting of Nomades, from the 5th to the 19th Century. Part IV. The Circassians and White Kazars. By H. H. Howorth.—Notes and Queries.—Illustrated.

Vol. II., No. 3. October, 1870. 8vo. pp. 176, sewed. 3*s*.

CONTENTS:—On the Aymara Indians of Bolivia and Peru. By David Forbes. Appendix: A. Table of Detailed Measurements of Aymara Indians. B. Substances used as Medicines by the Aymara Indians, and their Names for Diseases. C. Vocabulary of Aymara Words—Discussion.—On the Opening of Two Cairns near Bangor, North Wales. By Colonel A. Lane Fox.—Discussion.—On the Earliest Phases of Civilization. By Hodder M. Westropp.—On Current British Mythology and Oral Traditions. By J. F. Campbell.—Note on a Cist with Engraved Stones on the Poltalloch Estate, Argyllshire. By the Rev. R. J. Mapleton.—Discussion.—On the Tribal System and Land Tenure in Ireland under the Brehon Laws. By Hodder M. Westropp.—Discussion.—On the Danish Element in the Population of Cleveland, Yorkshire. By the Rev. J. C. Atkinson.—Discussion.—Notes and Queries.—Illustrated.

Vol. II., No. 4. January, 1871. 8vo. pp. 524, sewed. With a Coloured folded Map, and Seven full-page Illustrations. 3*s*.

CONTENTS.—On the Brain in the Study of Ethnology. By Dr. C. Donovan. (Abstract.)—The Philosophy of Religion among the Lower Races of Mankind. By E. B. Tylor, Esq., Vice-President (Discussion).—Address on the Ethnology of Britain. By Prof. T. H. Huxley, LL.D., F.R.S., President.—The Influence of the Norman Conquest on the Ethnology of Britain. By Dr. T. Nicholas, M.A., F.G.S. Discussion.—Note on a Supposed Ogham Inscription from Rus-Glass, Co. Cork. By R. Caulfield, Esq., LL.D., F.S.A. (with plate.) Discussion.—Notes on the Discovery of Copper Celts at Buttivant, Co. Cork. By J. P. Phair, Esq.—On the Geographical Distribution of the Chief Modifications of Mankind. By Prof. T. H. Huxley, LL.D., F.R.S., President (with chromo-lithograph map). Discussion.—On the threatened Destruction of the British Earthworks near Dorchester, Oxfordshire. By Col. A. Lane Fox, F.S.A., Hon. Sec. (with plate.)—Description of the Park Cwm Tumulus. By Sir John Lubbock, Bart., M.P., F.R.S., Vice-President (with plate).—On the Opening of Grimes' Graves in Norfolk. By the Rev. W. Greenwell, M.A., F.S.A. (with plates). Discussion.—On the Discovery of Platycnemic Men in Denbighshire. By W. Boyd Dawkins, Esq., M.A., F.R.S. With Notes on the Human Remains, by Prof. Busk, F.R.S. (with plate and 16 woodcuts.)—On the Westerly Drifting of Nomades, from the Fifth to the Nineteenth Century. Part V. The Hungarians. By H. H. Howorth, Esq.—Notes and Queries.—Index, &c., &c.

Facsimiles of Two Papyri found in a Tomb at Thebes. With a Translation by SAMUEL BIRCH, LL.D., F.S.A., Corresponding Member of the Institute of France, Academies of Berlin, Herculaneum, etc., and an Account of their Discovery. By A. HENRY RHIND, Esq., F.S.A., etc. In large folio, pp. 30 of text, and 16 plates coloured, bound in cloth. 21*s*.

Foss.—NORWEGIAN GRAMMAR, with Exercises in the Norwegian and and English Languages, and a List of Irregular Verbs. By FRITHJOF FOSS, Graduate of the University of Norway. Crown 8vo., pp. 50, cloth limp. 2*s*.

Furnivall.—EDUCATION IN EARLY ENGLAND. Some Notes used as Forewords to a Collection of Treatises on "Manners and Meals in the Olden Time," for the Early English Text Society. By FREDERICK J. FURNIVALL, M.A., Trinity Hall, Cambridge, Member of Council of the Philological and Early English Text Societies. 8vo. sewed, pp. 74. 1*s*.

Gesenius' Hebrew Grammar. Translated from the 17th Edition. By Dr. T. J. CONANT. With grammatical Exercises and a Chrestomathy by the Translator. 8vo. pp. xvi. and 364, cloth. 20*s*.

Gesenius' Hebrew and English Lexicon of the Old Testament, including the Biblical Chaldee, from the Latin. By EDWARD ROBINSON. Fifth Edition. 8vo. pp. xii. and 1160, cloth. 36*s*.

God.—BOOK OF GOD. By ☉. 8vo. cloth. Vol. I.: The Apocalypse. pp. 647. 12*s*. 6*d*.—Vol. II. An Introduction to the Apocalypse, pp. 752. 14*s*.—Vol. III. A Commentary on the Apocalypse, pp. 854. 16*s*.

God.—THE NAME OF GOD IN 405 LANGUAGES. Ἀγνώστῳ Θεῷ. 32mo. pp. 64, sewed. 2*d*.

Goldstücker.—A DICTIONARY, SANSKRIT AND ENGLISH, extended and improved from the Second Edition of the Dictionary of Professor H. H. WILSON, with his sanction and concurrence. Together with a Supplement, Grammatical Appendices, and an Index, serving as a Sanskrit-English Vocabulary. By THEODOR GOLDSTÜCKER. Parts I. to VI. 4to. pp. 400. 1856-1863. 6*s*. each.

Goldstücker.—A COMPENDIOUS SANSKRIT-ENGLISH DICTIONARY, for the Use of those who intend to read the easier Works of Classical Sanskrit Literature. By THEODOR GOLDSTÜCKER. Small 4to. pp. 900, cloth. [*In preparation.*

Goldstücker.—Panini: His Place in Sanskrit Literature. An Investigation of some Literary and Chronological Questions which may be settled by a study of his Work. A separate impression of the Preface to the Facsimile of MS. No. 17 in the Library of Her Majesty's Home Government for India, which contains a portion of the Manava-Kalpa-Sutra, with the Commentary of Kumarila-Swamin. By Theodor Goldstücker. Imperial 8vo. pp. 268, cloth. 12*s.*

Goldstücker.—On the Deficiencies in the Present Administration of Hindu Law; being a paper read at the Meeting of the East India Association on the 8th June, 1870. By Theodor Goldstücker, Professor of Sanskrit in University College, London, &c. Demy 8vo. pp. 56, sewed. 1*s.* 6*d.*

Grammatography.—A Manual of Reference to the Alphabets of Ancient and Modern Languages. Based on the German Compilation of F. Ballhorn. Royal 8vo. pp. 80, cloth. 7*s.* 6*d.*

The "Grammatography" is offered to the public as a compendious introduction to the reading of the most important ancient and modern languages. Simple in its design, it will be consulted with advantage by the philological student, the amateur linguist, the bookseller, the corrector of the press, and the diligent compositor.

ALPHABETICAL INDEX.

Afghan (or Pushto).
Amharic.
Anglo-Saxon.
Arabic.
Arabic Ligatures.
Aramaic.
Archaic Characters.
Armenian.
Assyrian Cuneiform.
Bengali.
Bohemian (Czechian).
Bugis.
Burmese.
Canarese (or Carnâtaca).
Chinese.
Coptic.
Croato-Glagolitic.
Cufic.
Cyrillic (or Old Slavonic).
Czechian (or Bohemian).
Danish.
Demotic.
Estrangelo.
Ethiopic.
Etruscan.
Georgian.
German.
Glagolitic.
Gothic.
Greek.
Greek Ligatures.
Greek (Archaic).
Gujerati (or Guzzeratte).
Hieratic.
Hieroglyphics.
Hebrew.
Hebrew (Archaic).
Hebrew (Rabbinical).
Hebrew (current hand).
Hebrew (Judæo-German).
Hungarian.
Illyrian.
Irish.
Italian (Old).
Japanese.
Javanese.
Lettish.
Mantshu.
Median Cuneiform.
Modern Greek (Romaic)
Mongolian.
Numidian.
Old Slavonic (or Cyrillic).
Palmyrenian.
Persian.
Persian Cuneiform.
Phœnician.
Polish.
Pushto (or Afghan).
Romaic (Modern Greek)
Russian.
Runes.
Samaritan.
Sanscrit.
Servian.
Slavonic (Old).
Sorbian (or Wendish).
Swedish.
Syriac.
Tamil.
Telugu.
Tibetan.
Turkish.
Wallachian.
Wendish (or Sorbian).
Zend.

Green.—Shakespeare and the Emblem-Writers: an Exposition of their Similarities of Thought and Expression. Preceded by a View of the Emblem-Book Literature down to A.D. 1616. By Henry Green, M.A. In one volume, pp. xvi. 572, profusely illustrated with Woodcuts and Photolith. Plates, elegantly bound in cloth gilt, large medium 8vo. £1 11*s.* 6*d*; large imperial 8vo. 1870. £2 12*s.* 6*d.*

Grey.—Handbook of African, Australian, and Polynesian Philology, as represented in the Library of His Excellency Sir George Grey, K.C.B., Her Majesty's High Commissioner of the Cape Colony. Classed, Annotated, and Edited by Sir George Grey and Dr. H. I. Bleek.

Vol. I. Part 1.—South Africa. 8vo. pp. 186. 7*s.* 6*d.*
Vol. I. Part 2.—Africa (North of the Tropic of Capricorn). 8vo. pp. 70. 2*s.*
Vol. I. Part 3.—Madagascar. 8vo. pp. 24. 1*s.*
Vol. II. Part 1.—Australia. 8vo. pp. iv. and 44. 1*s.* 6*d.*
Vol. II. Part 2.—Papuan Languages of the Loyalty Islands and New Hebrides, comprising those of the Islands of Nengone, Lifu, Aneitum, Tana, and others. 8vo. p. 12. 6*d.*
Vol. II. Part 3.—Fiji Islands and Rotuma (with Supplement to Part II., Papuan Languages, and Part I., Australia). 8vo. pp. 34. 1*s.*
Vol. II. Part 4.—New Zealand, the Chatham Islands, and Auckland Islands. 8vo. pp. 76. 3*s.* 6*d.*
Vol. II. Part 4 (*continuation*).—Polynesia and Borneo. 8vo. pp. 77-154. 3*s.* 6*d.*
Vol. III. Part 1.—Manuscripts and Incunables. 8vo. pp. viii. and 24. 2*s.*
Vol. IV. Part 1.—Early Printed Books. England. 8vo. pp. vi. and 266.

Grey.—Maori Mementos: being a Series of Addresses presented by the Native People to His Excellency Sir George Grey, K.C.B., F.R.S. With Introductory Remarks and Explanatory Notes; to which is added a small Collection of Laments, etc. By Ch. Oliver B. Davis. 8vo. pp. iv. and 228, cloth. 12*s.*

Griffith.—Scenes from the Ramayana, Meghaduta, etc. Translated by Ralph T. H. Griffith, M.A., Principal of the Benares College. Second Edition. Crown 8vo. pp. xviii., 244, cloth. 6*s.*

Contents.—Preface—Ayodhya—Ravan Doomed—The Birth of Rama—The Heir apparent—Manthara's Guile—Dasaratha's Oath—The Step-mother—Mother and Son—The Triumph of Love—Farewell?—The Hermit's Son—The Trial of Truth—The Forest—The Rape of Sita—Rama's Despair—The Messenger Cloud—Khumbakarna—The Suppliant Dove—True Glory—Feed the Poor—The Wise Scholar.

Griffith.—The Rámáyan of Válmíki. Translated into English verse. By Ralph T. H. Griffith, M.A., Principal of the Benares College. Vol. I., containing Books I. and II. 8vo. pp. xxxii. 440, cloth. 1870. 18*s.*

——— Vol. II., containing Book II., with additional Notes and Index of Names. 8vo. cloth, pp. 504. 18*s.*

Grout.—The Isizulu: a Grammar of the Zulu Language; accompanied with an Historical Introduction, also with an Appendix. By Rev. Lewis Grout. 8vo. pp. lii. and 432, cloth. 21*s.*

Gubernatis.—Mythical Zoology; or the Legends of Animals. By Angelo de Gubernatis, Professor of Sanskrit and Comparative Literature at Florence. [*In the press.*

Gundert.—A Malayalam and English Dictionary. By Rev. H. Gundert, D.Ph. Part I: The Vowels. Royal 8vo. pp. 192, sewed. 1871. 10*s.*

Haldeman.—A Grammar of the Pennsylvanian Dutch Language. By S. S. Haldeman. 8vo. [*In the Press.*

Hans Breitmann Ballads.—See under Leland.

Haug.—Essays on the Sacred Language, Writings, and Religion of the Parsees. By Martin Haug, Dr. Phil. Superintendent of Sanskrit Studies in the Poona College. 8vo. pp. 278, cloth. [*Out of print.*

Haug.—A Lecture on an Original Speech of Zoroaster (Yasna 45), with remarks on his age. By Martin Haug, Ph.D. 8vo. pp. 28, sewed. Bombay, 1865. 2*s.*

Haug.—Outline of a Grammar of the Zend Language. By Martin Haug, Dr. Phil. 8vo. pp. 82, sewed. 14*s.*

Haug.—The Aitareya Brahmanam of the Rig Veda: containing the Earliest Speculations of the Brahmans on the meaning of the Sacrificial Prayers, and on the Origin, Performance, and Sense of the Rites of the Vedic Religion. Edited, Translated, and Explained by Martin Haug, Ph.D., Superintendent of Sanskrit Studies in the Poona College, etc., etc. In 2 Vols. Crown 8vo. Vol. I. Contents, Sanskrit Text, with Preface, Introductory Essay, and a Map of the Sacrificial Compound at the Soma Sacrifice, pp. 312. Vol. II. Translation with Notes, pp. 544. £3 3*s.*

Haug.—An Old Zand-Pahlavi Glossary. Edited in the Original Characters, with a Transliteration in Roman Letters, an English Translation, and an Alphabetical Index. By Destur Hoshengji Jamaspji, High-priest of the Parsis in Malwa, India. Revised with Notes and Introduction by Martin Haug, Ph.D., late Superintendent of Sanscrit Studies in the Poona College, Foreign Member of the Royal Bavarian Academy. Published by order of the Government of Bombay. 8vo. sewed, pp. lvi. and 132. 15*s.*

Haug.—An Old Pahlavi-Pazand Glossary. Edited, with an Alphabetical Index, by Destur Hoshangji Jamaspji Asa, High Priest of the Parsis in Malwa, India. Revised and Enlarged, with an Introductory Essay on the Pahlavi Language, by Martin Haug, Ph.D. Published by order of the Government of Bombay. 8vo. pp. xvi. 152, 268, sewed. 1870. 28*s.*

Haug.—Essay on the Pahlavi Language. By Martin Haug, Ph. D., Professor of Sanscrit and Comparative Philology at the University of Munich, Member of the Royal Bavarian Academy of Sciences, etc. (From the Pahlavi-Pazand Glossary, edited by Destur Hoshangji and M. Haug.) 8vo. pp. 152, sewed. 1870. 3*s.* 6*d.*

Haug.—THE RELIGION OF THE ZOROASTRIANS, as contained in their Sacred Writings. With a History of the Zend and Pehlevi Literature, and a Grammar of the Zend and Pehlevi Languages. By MARTIN HAUG, Ph.D., late Superintendent of Sanscrit Studies in the Poona College. 2 vols. 8vo. [*In preparation.*

Heaviside.—AMERICAN ANTIQUITIES; or, the New World the Old, and the Old World the New. By JOHN T. C. HEAVISIDE. 8vo. pp. 46, sewed. 1*s.* 6*d.*

Hepburn.—A JAPANESE AND ENGLISH DICTIONARY. With an English and Japanese Index. By J. C. HEPBURN, A.M., M.D. Imperial 8vo. cloth, pp. xii., 560 and 132. 5*l.* 5*s.*

Hernisz.—A GUIDE TO CONVERSATION IN THE ENGLISH AND CHINESE LANGUAGES, for the use of Americans and Chinese in California and elsewhere. By STANISLAS HERNISZ. Square 8vo. pp. 274, sewed. 10*s.* 6*d.*

The Chinese characters contained in this work are from the collections of Chinese groups, engraved on steel, and cast into moveable types, by Mr. Marcellin Legrand, engraver of the Imperial Printing Office at Paris. They are used by most of the missions to China.

Hincks.—SPECIMEN CHAPTERS OF AN ASSYRIAN GRAMMAR. By the late Rev. E. HINCKS, D.D., Hon. M.R.A.S. 8vo., pp. 44, sewed. 1*s.*

History of the Sect of Maharajahs; or, VALLABHACHARYAS IN WESTERN INDIA. With a Steel Plate. 8vo. pp. 384, cloth. 12*s.*

Hoffmann.—SHOPPING DIALOGUES, in Japanese, Dutch, and English. By Professor J. HOFFMANN. Oblong 8vo. pp. xiii. and 44, sewed. 3*s.*

Hoffmann.—A JAPANESE GRAMMAR. By J. J. HOFFMANN, Ph. Doc., Member of the Royal Academy of Sciences, etc., etc. Published by command of His Majesty's Minister for Colonial Affairs. Imp. 8vo. pp. viii. 352, sewed. 12*s.* 6*d.*

Historia y fundacion de la Ciudad de Tlaxcala, y sus cuatro caveceras. Sacada por Francisco de Loaiza de lengua Castellana à esta Mexicana. Año de 1718. Con una Traduccion Castellana, publicado por S. Leon Reinisch. In one volume folio, with 25 Photographic Plates. [*In preparation.*

Howse.—A GRAMMAR OF THE CREE LANGUAGE. With which is combined an analysis of the Chippeway Dialect. By JOSEPH HOWSE, Esq., F.R.G.S. 8vo. pp. xx. and 324, cloth. 7*s.* 6*d.*

Hunter.—A COMPARATIVE DICTIONARY OF THE LANGUAGES OF INDIA AND HIGH ASIA, with a Dissertation, based on The Hodgson Lists, Official Records, and Manuscripts. By W. W. HUNTER, B.A., M.R.A.S., Honorary Fellow, Ethnological Society, of Her Majesty's Bengal Civil Service. Folio, pp. vi. and 224, cloth. £2 2*s.*

Ikhwánu-s Safá.—IKHWÁNU-S SAFÁ; or, BROTHERS OF PURITY. Describing the Contention between Men and Beasts as to the Superiority of the Human Race. Translated from the Hindustání by Professor J. DOWSON, Staff College, Sandhurst. Crown 8vo. pp. viii. and 156, cloth. 7*s.*

Inman.—ANCIENT FAITHS EMBODIED IN ANCIENT TIMES; or, an attempt to trace the Religious Belief, Sacred Rites, and Holy Emblems of certain Nations, by an interpretation of the names given to children by Priestly authority, or assumed by prophets, kings and hierarchs. By THOMAS INMAN, M.D., Liverpool. 2 vols. 8vo. pp. l. and 1028, cloth, illustrated with numerous plates and woodcuts. £3.

Inman.—ANCIENT PAGAN AND MODERN CHRISTIAN SYMBOLISM EXPOSED AND EXPLAINED. By THOMAS INMAN, M.D. (London), Physician to the Royal Infirmary, Liverpool. 8vo. pp. xvi. 68, stiff covers, with numerous Illustrations. 1870. 5*s.*

Jaeschke.—A SHORT PRACTICAL GRAMMAR OF THE TIBETAN LANGUAGE, with special Reference to the Spoken Dialects. By H. A. JAESCHKE, Moravian Missionary. 8vo sewed, pp. ii. and 56. 2*s.* 6*d.*

Jaeschke.—ROMANIZED TIBETAN AND ENGLISH DICTIONARY, each word being re-produced in the Tibetan as well as in the Roman character. By H. A. JAESCHKE, Moravian Missionary. 8vo. pp. ii. and 158, sewed. 5*s.*

Jaiminiya-Nyâya-Mâlâ-Vistara.—See under AUCTORES SANSCRITI.

Jenkins's Vest-Pocket Lexicon.—AN ENGLISH DICTIONARY of all except Familiar Words; including the principal Scientific and Technical Terms, and Foreign Moneys, Weights and Measures. By JABEZ JENKINS. 64mo., pp. 564, cloth. 1*s*. 6*d*.

Julien.—SYNTAXE NOUVELLE DE LA LANGUE CHINOISE.

Vol. I.—Fondée sur la position des mots, suivie de deux traités sur les particules et les principaux termes de grammaire, d'une table des idiotismes, de fables, de légendes et d'apologues traduits mot à mot. 8vo. sewed. 1869. 20*s*.

Vol. II.—Fondée sur la position des mots confirmée par l'analyse d'un texte ancien, suivie d'un petit Dictionnaire du Roman des DEUX COUSINES, et de Dialogues dramatiques traduits mot à mot, par M. STANISLAS JULIEN, de l'Institut. 8vo. pp. 436, sewed. 1870. 20*s*.

Justi.—HANDBUCH DER ZENDSPRACHE, VON FERDINAND JUSTI. Altbactrisches Woerterbuch. Grammatik Chrestomathie. Four parts, 4to. sewed, pp. xxii. and 424. Leipzig, 1864. 24s.

Kachchayano's Grammar (**The Pali Text of**), with ENGLISH GRAMMAR. See under MASON.

Kafir Essays, and other Pieces; with an English Translation. Edited by the Right Rev. the BISHOP OF GRAHAMSTOWN. 32mo. pp. 84, sewed. 2*s* 6*d*.

Kalidasa.—RAGHUVANSA. By KALIDASA. No. 1. (Cantos 1-3.) With Notes and Grammatical Explanations, by Rev. K. M. BANERJEA, Second Professor of Bishop's College, Calcutta; Member of the Board of Examiners, Fort-William; Honorary Member of the Royal Asiatic Society, London. 8vo. sewed, pp. 70. 4*s*. 6*d*.

Kern.—THE BRHAT-SANHITÁ; or, Complete System of Natural Astrology of Varâha-Mihira. Translated from Sanskrit into English by Dr. H. KERN, Professor of Sanskrit at the University of Leyden. 8vo. pp. 50, stitched, Part I. 2*s*. [*Will be completed in Nine Parts.*

Khirad-Afroz (The Illuminator of the Understanding). By Maulaví Hafízu'd-dín. A new edition of the Hindústání Text, carefully revised, with Notes, Critical and Explanatory. By EDWARD B. EASTWICK, M.P., F.R.S., F.S.A., M.R.A.S., Professor of Hindústání at the late East India Company's College at Haileybury. 8vo. cloth, pp. xiv. and 321. 18*s*.

Khuddaka Patha.—See under CHILDERS.

Kidd.—CATALOGUE OF THE CHINESE LIBRARY OF THE ROYAL ASIATIC SOCIETY. By the Rev. S. KIDD. 8vo. pp. 58, sewed. 1*s*.

Kielhorn.—A GRAMMAR OF THE SANSKRIT LANGUAGE. By F. KIELHORN, Ph.D., Superintendent of Sanskrit Studies in Deccan College. Registered under Act xxv. of 1867. Demy 8vo. pp. xvi. 260. cloth. 1870. 10*s*. 6*d*.

Kistner.—BUDDHA AND HIS DOCTRINES. A Bibliographical Essay. By OTTO KISTNER. Imperial 8vo., pp. iv. and 32, sewed. 2*s*. 6*d*.

Koran (The). Arabic text, lithographed in Oudh, A.H. 1284 (1867). 16mo. pp. 942, bound in red goatskin, Oriental style, silver tooling. 7*s*. 6*d*.

The printing, as well as the outer appearance of the book, is extremely tasteful, and the characters, although small, read very easily. As a cheap edition for reference this is preferable to any other, and its price puts it within the reach of every Oriental scholar. It is now first imported from India.

Laghu Kaumudí. A Sanskrit Grammar. By Varadarája. With an English Version, Commentary, and References. By JAMES R. BALLANTYNE, LL.D., Principal of the Snskrit College, Benares. 8vo. pp. xxxvi. and 424, cloth. £1 11*s*. 6*d*.

Lee.—A TRANSLATION OF THE BÁLÁVATÁRO: a Native Grammar of the Pali Language. With the Romanized Text, the Nagari Text, and Copious Explanatory Notes. By LIONEL F. LEE. In one vol. 8vo. (*In preparation*).

Legge.—The Chinese Classics. With a Translation, Critical and Exegetical Notes, Prolegomena, and Copious Indexes. By James Legge, D.D., of the London Missionary Society. In seven vols.

Vol. I. containing Confucian Analects, the Great Learning, and the Doctrine of the Mean. 8vo. pp. 526, cloth. £2 2*s*.

Vol. II., containing the Works of Mencius. 8vo. pp. 634, cloth. £2 2*s*.

Vol. III. Part I. containing the First Part of the Shoo-King, or the Books of Tang, the Books of Yu, the Books of Hea, the Books of Shang, and the Prolegomena. Royal 8vo. pp. viii. and 280, cloth. £2 2*s*.

Vol. III. Part II. containing the Fifth Part of the Shoo-King, or the Books of Chow, and the Indexes. Royal 8vo. pp. 281—736, cloth. £2 2*s*.

Legge.—The Life and Teachings of Confucius, with Explanatory Notes. By James Legge, D.D. Reproduced for General Readers from the Author's work, "The Chinese Classics," with the original Text. Second edition. Crown 8vo. cloth, pp. vi. and 338. 10*s*. 6*d*.

Leigh.—The Religion of the World. By H. Stone Leigh. 12mo. pp. xii. 66, cloth. 1869. 2*s*. 6*d*.

Leitner.—The Races and Languages of Dardistan. By G. W. Leitner, M.A., Ph.D., Honorary Fellow of King's College London, etc.; late on Special Duty in Kashmir. Parts 1 and 2.—5*s*. each.

Leland.—The Breitmann Ballads. The only Authorized Edition. Complete in 1 vol., including Nineteen Ballads illustrating his Travels in Europe (never before printed), with Comments by Fritz Schwackenhammer. By Charles G. Leland. Crown 8vo. handsomely bound in cloth, pp. xxviii. and 292. 6*s*.

Hans Breitmann's Party. With other Ballads. By Charles G. Leland. Tenth Edition. Square, pp. xvi. and 74, sewed. 1*s*.

Hans Breitmann's Christmas. With other Ballads. By Charles G. Leland. Second edition. Square, pp. 80, sewed. 1*s*.

Hans Breitmann as a Politician. By Charles G. Leland. Second edition. Square, pp. 72, sewed. 1*s*.

Hans Breitmann in Church. With other Ballads. By Charles G. Leland. With an Introduction and Glossary. Second edition. Square, pp. 80, sewed. 1870. 1*s*.

Hans Breitmann as an Uhlan. Six New Ballads, with a Glossary. Square, pp. 72, sewed. 1*s*.

The first four Parts may be had in one Volume:—

Breitmann Ballads. *Four Series complete.* Contents:—Hans Breitmann's Party. Hans Breitmann's Christmas. Hans Breitmann as a Politician. Hans Breitmann in Church. With other Ballads. By Charles G. Leland. With Introductions and Glossaries. Square, pp. 300, cloth. 1870. 4*s*. 6*d*.

Lesley.—Man's Origin and Destiny, Sketched from the Platform of the Sciences, in a Course of Lectures delivered before the Lowell Institute, in Boston, in the Winter of 1865-6. By J. P. Lesley, Member of the National Academy of the United States, Secretary of the American Philosophical Society. Numerous Woodcuts. Crown 8vo. pp. 392, cloth. 10*s*. 6*d*.

Liherien hag Avielen; or, the Catholic Epistles and Gospels for the Day up to Ascension. Translated for the first time into the Brehonec of Brittany. Also in three other parallel columns a New Version of the same into Breizounec (commonly called Breton and Armorican); a Version into Welsh, mostly new, and closely resembling the Breton; and a Version Gaelic or Manx or Cernaweg; with Illustrative Articles by Christoll Terrien and Charles Waring Saxton, D.D. Ch. Ch., Oxford. The Penitential Psalms are also added. Oblong 4to. pp. 156, sewed. 5*s*.

Lobscheid.—ENGLISH AND CHINESE DICTIONARY, with the Punti and Mandarin Pronunciation. By the Rev. W. LOBSCHEID, Knight of Francis Joseph, C.M.I.R.G.S.A., N.Z.B.S.V., etc. Folio, pp. viii. and 2016. In Four Parts. £8 8*s.*

Lobscheid.—CHINESE AND ENGLISH DICTIONARY, Arranged according to the Radicals. By the Rev. W. LOBSCHEID, Knight of Francis Joseph, C.M.I.R.G.S.A., N.Z.B.S.V., &c. 1 vol. imp. 8vo. double columns, pp. 600, bound. £2 8*s.*

Ludewig (Hermann E.)—The LITERATURE of AMERICAN ABORIGINAL LANGUAGES. With Additions and Corrections by Professor WM. W. TURNER. Edited by NICOLAS TRÜBNER. 8vo. fly and general Title, 2 leaves; Dr. Ludewig's Preface, pp. v.—viii.; Editor's Preface, pp. iv.—xii.; Biographical Memoir of Dr. Ludewig, pp. xiii.—xiv.; and Introductory Biographical Notices, pp. xiv.—xxiv., followed by List of Contents. Then follow Dr. Ludewig's Bibliotheca Glottica, alphabetically arranged, with Additions by the Editor, pp. 1—209; Professor Turner's Additions, with those of the Editor to the same, also alphabetically arranged, pp. 210—246; Index, pp. 247—256; and List of Errata, pp. 257, 258. Handsomely bound in cloth. 10*s.* 6*d.*

Macgowan.—A MANUAL OF THE AMOY COLLOQUIAL. By Rev. J. MACGOWAN, of the London Missionary Society. 8vo. sewed, pp. xvii. and 200. Amoy, 1871. £1 1*s.*

Maclay and Baldwin.—AN ALPHABETIC DICTIONARY OF THE CHINESE LANGUAGE IN THE FOOCHOW DIALECT. By Rev. R. S. MACLAY, D.D., of the Methodist Episcopal Mission, and Rev. C. C. BALDWIN, A.M., of the American Board of Mission. 8vo. half-bound, pp. 1132. Foochow, 1871. £4 4*s.*

Maha-Vira-Charita; or, the Adventures of the Great Hero Rama. An Indian Drama in Seven Acts. Translated into English Prose from the Sanskrit of Bhavabhûti. By JOHN PICKFORD, M.A. Crown 8vo. cloth. 5*s.*

Maino-i-Khard (The Book of the).—The Pazand and Sanskrit Texts (in Roman characters) as arranged by Neriosengh Dhaval, in the fifteenth century. With an English translation, a Glossary of the Pazand texts, containing the Sanskrit, Rosian, and Pahlavi equivalents, a sketch of Pazand Grammar, and an Introduction. By E. W. WEST. 8vo. sewed, pp. 484. 1871. 16*s.*

Manava-Kalpa-Sutra; being a portion of this ancient Work on Vaidik Rites, together with the Commentary of KUMARILA-SWAMIN. A Facsimile of the MS. No. 17, in the Library of Her Majesty's Home Government for India. With a Preface by THEODOR GOLDSTÜCKER. Oblong folio, pp. 268 of letter-press and 121 leaves of facsimiles. Cloth. £4 4*s.*

Manipulus Vocabulorum; A Rhyming Dictionary of the English Language. By Peter Levins (1570) Edited, with an Alphabetical Index, by HENRY B. WHEATLEY. 8vo, pp. xvi. and 370, cloth. 14*s.*

Manning.—AN INQUIRY INTO THE CHARACTER AND ORIGIN OF THE POSSESSIVE AUGMENT in English and in Cognate Dialects. By the late JAMES MANNING, Q.A.S., Recorder of Oxford. 8vo.pp. iv. and 90. 2*s.*

Markham.—QUICHUA GRAMMAR and DICTIONARY. Contributions towards a Grammar and Dictionary of Quichua, the Language of the Yncas of Peru; collected by CLEMENTS R. MARKHAM, F.S.A., Corr. Mem. of the University of Chile. Author of "Cuzco and Lima," and "Travels in Peru and India." In one vol. crown 8vo., pp. 223, cloth. £1. 1*s.*

Markham.—OLLANTA: A DRAMA IN THE QUICHUA LANGUAGE. Text, Translation, and Introduction, By CLEMENTS R. MARKHAM, F.R.G.S. Crown 8vo., pp. 128, cloth. 7*s.* 6*d.*

Marsden.—NUMISMATA ORIENTALIA ILLUSTRATA. The Plates of the Oriental Coins, Ancient and Modern, of the Collection of the late William Marsden, F.R.S., etc., etc., engraved from drawings made under his direction. 4to. pp. iv. (explanatory advertisement). cloth, gilt top. £1 11*s.* 6*d.*

Mason.—BURMAH: its People and Natural Productions; or Notes on the Nations, Fauna, Flora, and Minerals of Tenasserim, Pegu, and Burmah. By Rev. F. MASON, D.D., M.R.A.S., Corresponding Member of the American Oriental Society, of the Boston Society of Natural History, and of the Lyceum of Natural History, New York. 8vo. pp. xviii. and 914, cloth. Rangoon, 1860. 30*s*.

Mason.—THE PALI TEXT OF KACHCHAYANO'S GRAMMAR, WITH ENGLISH ANNOTATIONS. By FRANCIS MASON, D.D. I. The Text Aphorisms, 1 to 673. II. The English Annotations, including the various Readings of six independent Burmese Manuscripts, the Singalese Text on Verbs, and the Cambodian Text on Syntax. To which is added a Concordance of the Aphorisms. In Two Parts. 8vo. sewed, pp. 208, 75, and 28. Toongoo, 1871. £1 11*s*. 6*d*.

Mathurápraśáda Misra.—A TRILINGUAL DICTIONARY, being a comprehensive Lexicon in English, Urdú, and Hindí, exhibiting the Syllabication, Pronunciation, and Etymology of English Words, with their Explanation in English, and in Urdú and Hindí in the Roman Character. By MATHURÁPRASÁDA MISRA, Second Master, Queen's College, Benares. 8vo. pp. xv. and 1330, cloth. Benares, 1865. £2 2*s*.

Mayers.—ILLUSTRATIONS OF THE LAMAIST SYSTEM IN TIBET, drawn from Chinese Sources. By WILLIAM FREDERICK MAYERS, Esq., of Her Britannic Majesty's Consular Service, China. 8vo. pp. 24, sewed. 1869. 1*s*. 6*d*.

Medhurst.—CHINESE DIALOGUES, QUESTIONS, and FAMILIAR SENTENCES, literally translated into English, with a view to promote commercial intercourse and assist beginners in the Language. By the late W. H. MEDHURST, D.D. A new and enlarged Edition. 8vo. pp. 226. 18*s*.

Megha-Duta (The). (Cloud-Messenger.) By Kālidāsa. Translated from the Sanskrit into English verse, with Notes and Illustrations. By the late H. H. WILSON, M.A., F.R.S., Boden Professor of Sanskrit in the University of Oxford, etc., etc. The Vocabulary by FRANCIS JOHNSON, sometime Professor of Oriental Languages at the College of the Honourable the East India Company, Haileybury. New Edition. 4to. cloth, pp. xi. and 180. 10*s*. 6*d*.

Memoirs read before the ANTHROPOLOGICAL SOCIETY OF LONDON, 1863 1864. 8vo., pp. 542, cloth. 21*s*.

Memoirs read before the ANTHROPOLOGICAL SOCIETY OF LONDON, 1865-6. Vol. II. 8vo., pp. x. 464, cloth. 21*s*.

Moffat.—THE STANDARD ALPHABET PROBLEM; or the Preliminary Subject of a General Phonic System, considered on the basis of some important facts in the Sechwana Language of South Africa, and in reference to the views of Professors Lepsius, Max Müller, and others. A contribution to Phonetic Philology. By ROBERT MOFFAT, junr., Surveyor, Fellow of the Royal Geographical Society. 8vo. pp. xxviii. and 174, cloth. 7*s*. 6*d*.

Molesworth.—A DICTIONARY, MÁRATHI and ENGLISH. Compiled by J. T. MOLESWORTH, assisted by GEORGE and THOMAS CANDY. Second Edition, revised and enlarged. By J. T. MOLESWORTH. Royal 4to. pp. xxx. and 922, boards. Bombay, 1857. £3 3*s*.

Molesworth.—A COMPENDIUM OF MOLESWORTH'S MARATHI AND ENGLISH DICTIONARY. By BABA PADMANJI. Small 4to., pp. xii. and 482, cloth. 16*s*.

Morfill.—THE SLAVES: their Ethnology, early History, and popular Traditions, with some account of Slavonic Literature. Being the substance of a course of Lectures delivered at Oxford. By W. R. MORFILL, M.A.
[*In preparation*.

Morley.—A DESCRIPTIVE CATALOGUE of the HISTORICAL MANUSCRIPTS in the ARABIC and PERSIAN LANGUAGES preserved in the Library of the Royal Asiatic Society of Great Britain and Ireland. By WILLIAM H. MORLEY, M.R.A.S. 8vo. pp. viii. and 160, sewed. London, 1854. 2*s*. 6*d*.

Morrison.—A DICTIONARY OF THE CHINESE LANGUAGE. By the Rev. R. MORRISON, D.D. Two vols. Vol. I. pp. x. and 762; Vol. II. pp. 828, cloth. Shanghae, 1865. £6 6*s*.

Muhammed.—THE LIFE OF MUHAMMED. Based on Muhammed Ibn Ishak. By Abd El Malik Ibn Hisham. Edited by Dr. FERDINAND WÜSTENFELD. One volume containing the Arabic Text. 8vo. pp. 1026, sewed. Price 21*s*. Another volume, containing Introduction, Notes, and Index in German. 8vo. pp. lxxii. and 266, sewed. 7*s*. 6*d*. Each part sold separately

The text based on the Manuscripts of the Berlin, Leipsic, Gotha and Leyden Libraries, has been carefully revised by the learned editor, and printed with the utmost exactness.

Muir.—ORIGINAL SANSKRIT TEXTS, on the Origin and History of the People of India, their Religion and Institutions. Collected, Translated, and Illustrated by JOHN MUIR, Esq., D.C.L., LL.D., Ph.D.

Vol. I. Mythical and Legendary Accounts of the Origin of Caste, with an Inquiry into its existence in the Vedic Age. Second Edition, re-written and greatly enlarged. 8vo. pp. xx. 532, cloth. 1868. 21*s*.

Vol. II. The Trans-Himalayan Origin of the Hindus, and their Affinity with the Western Branches of the Aryan Race. Second Edition, revised, with Additions. 8vo. pp. xxxii. and 512, cloth. 12*s*.

Second Edition. 8vo. pp. xxxii., 512. 1871. 21*s*.

Vol. III. The Vedas: Opinions of their Authors, and of later Indian Writers, on their Origin, Inspiration, and Authority. Second Edition, revised and enlarged. 8vo. pp. xxxii. 312, cloth. 1868. (16*s*.) Rs. 8.

Vol. IV. Comparison of the Vedic with the later representation of the principal Indian Deities. 8vo. pp. xii. 440, cloth. 1863. 15*s*. (Out of print. A second edition is preparing.)

Vol. V. Contributions to a Knowledge of the Cosmogony, Mythology, Religious Ideas, Life and Manners of the Indians in the Vedic Age. 8vo. pp. xvi. 492, cloth, 1870. 21*s*.

Müller.—THE SACRED HYMNS OF THE BRAHMINS, as preserved to us in the oldest collection of religious poetry, the Rig-Veda-Sanhita, translated and explained. By F. MAX MÜLLER, M.A., Fellow of All Souls' College; Professor of Comparative Philology at Oxford; Foreign Member of the Institute of France, etc., etc. In 8 vols. Volume I. 8vo. pp. clii. and 264. 12*s*. 6*d*.

Müller.—A NEW EDITION OF THE HYMNS OF THE RIG-VEDA IN THE SANHITÁ TEXT, without the Commentary of the Sáyana. Based upon the Editio princeps of Max Müller. Large 8vo. of about 800 pages. [*In preparation.*

"The above New Edition of the Sanhitá Text of the Rig-Veda, without the Commentary of Sáyana, will contain foot-notes of the names of the Authors, Deities, and Metres. It will be comprised in about fifty large 8vo. sheets, and will be carefully corrected and revised by Prof. F. Max Müller. The price to subscribers before publication will be 24*s*. per copy. After publication the price will be 36*s*. per copy.

Müller.—LECTURE ON BUDDHIST NIHILISM. By F. MAX MÜLLER, M.A., Professor of Comparative Philology in the University of Oxford; Member of the French Institute, etc. Delivered before the General Meeting of the Association of German Philologists, at Kiel, 28th September, 1869. (Translated from the German.) Sewed. 1869. 1*s*.

Nagananda.—A DRAMA TRANSLATED FROM THE ORIGINAL SANSKRIT; with Notes, by PALMER BOYD, B.A., Trinity Hall. With a Preface by Prof. E. B. COWELL, Cambridge. Crown 8vo. [*In the Press.*

Naphegyi.—THE ALBUM OF LANGUAGE, illustrated by the Lord's Prayer in one hundred languages, with historical descriptions of the principal languages, interlinear translation and pronunciation of each prayer, a dissertation on the languages of the world, and tables exhibiting all known languages, dead and living. By G. NAPHEGYI, M.D., A.M., Member of the "Sociedad Geográfica y Estadistica" of Mexico, and "Mejoras Materiales" of Texoco, of the Numismatic and Antiquarian Society of Philadelphia, etc. In one splendid folio volume of 322 pages, illuminated frontispiece and title-page, elegantly bound in cloth, gilt top. £2 10*s*.

CONTENTS.—Preface (pp. 2).—Introduction.—Observations on the Origin of Language (pp. 12).—Authors of Collections of the Lord's Prayer (pp. 8).—Families of Language (pp. 18).—Alphabets (pp. 25). The Lord's Prayer in the following languages (each accompanied by a transliteration into Roman characters, a translation into English, and a Monograph of the language), printed in the original characters.

A. Aryan Family.—1. Sanskrit. 2. Bengalee. 3. Moltanee. 4. Hindoostanee. 5. Gipsy. 6. Greek. 7. Modern Greek. 8. Latin. 9. Italian. 10. French. 11. Spanish. 12. Portuguese. 13. Celtic. 14. Welsh. 15. Cornish. 16. Irish. 17. Gothic. 18. Anglo-Saxon. 19. Old Saxon and Dano-Saxon. 20. English (4 varieties). 21. German (4 varieties). 22. Dutch. 23. Runic. 24. Wallachian. 25. Icelandic. 26. Danish. 27. Norwegian. 28. Swedish. 29 Lithuanian. 30. Old Prussian. 31. Servian. 32. Sclavonic. 33. Polavian. 34. Bohemian. 35. Polish. 36. Russian. 37. Bulgaric. 38. Armenian. 39. Armenian-Turkish. 40. Albanian. 41. Persian.

B. Semitic Family.—1. Hebrew. 2. Chaldee. 3. Samaritan. 4. Syriac. 5. Syro-Chaldæic. 6. Carshun. 7. Arabic. 8. Æthiopic. 8. Amharic.

C. Turanian Family.—1. Turkish. 2. Hungarian. 3. Finnish. 4. Estonian. 5. Lapponian. 6. Laplandic (Dialect of Umä-Lappmark). 7. Basque. 8. Javanese. 9. Hawaiian. 10. Maori (New Zealandic). 11. Malay. 12. Ceylonese. 13. Moorish. 14. Coptic. 15. Berber. 16. Hottentot. 17. Susuic. 18. Burmese. 19. Siamese. 20. Mongolian. 21. Chinese. 22. Kalmuk. 23. Cashmere.

D. American Family.—1. Cherokee. 2. Delawar. 3. Micmac. 4. Totonac. 5. Othomi. 6. Cora. 7. Kolusic. 8. Greenland. 9. Mexican. 10. Mistekic. 11. Mayu. 12. Brasilian. 13. Chiquitic. 14. Amaric.

Nayler.—Commonsense Observations on the Existence of Rules (not yet reduced to System in any work extant) regarding The English Language; on the pernicious effects of yielding blind obedience to so-called authorities, whether Dictionary-Compilers, Grammar-Makers, or Spelling-Book Manufacturers, instead of examining and judging for ourselves on all questions that are open to investigation; followed by a Treatise, entitled Pronunciation made Easy; also an Essay on the Pronunciation of Proper Names. By B. S. Nayler, accredited Elocutionist to the most celebrated Literary Societies in London. 8vo. pp. iv. 148, boards. 1869. 5*s*.

Newman.—A Dictionary of Modern Arabic.—1. Anglo-Arabic Dictionary. 2. Anglo-Arabic Vocabulary. 3. Arabo-English Dictionary. By F. W. Newman, Emeritus Professor of University College, London. In 2 vols. crown 8vo., pp. xvi. and 376—464, cloth. £1 1*s*.

Newman.—A Handbook of Modern Arabic, consisting of a Practical Grammar, with numerous Examples, Dialogues, and Newspaper Extracts, in a European Type. By F. W. Newman, Emeritus Professor of University College, London; formerly Fellow of Balliol College, Oxford. Post 8vo. pp. xx. and 192, cloth. London, 1866. 6*s*.

Newman.—The Text of the Iguvine Inscriptions, with interlinear Latin Translation and Notes. By Francis W. Newman, late Professor of Latin at University College, London. 8vo. pp. xvi. and 54, sewed. 2*s*.

Newman.—Orthoëpy: or, a simple mode of Accenting English, for the advantage of Foreigners and of all Learners. By Francis W. Newman, Emeritus Professor of University College, London. 8vo. pp. 28, sewed. 1869. 1*s*.

Notley.—A Comparative Grammar of the French, Italian, Spanish, and Portuguese Languages. By Edwin A. Notley. Crown oblong 8vo. cloth, pp. xv. and 396. 7*s*. 6*d*.

Ollanta: A Drama in the Quichua Lanuuage. See under Markham.

Oriental Text Society.—(*The Publications of the Oriental Text Society.*)

1. Theophania; or, Divine Manifestations of our Lord and Saviour. By Eusebius, Bishop of Cæsarea. Syriac. Edited by Prof. S. Lee. 8vo. 1842. 15*s*.
2. Athanasius's Festal Letters, discovered in an ancient Syriac Version. Edited by the Rev. W. Cureton. 8vo. 1848. 15*s*.
3. Shahrastani: Book of Religious and Philosophical Sects, in Arabic. Two Parts. 8vo. 1842. 30*s*.
4. Umdat Akidat Ahl al Sunnat wa al Tamaat; Pillar of the Creed of the Sunnites. Edited in Arabic by the Rev. W. Cureton. 8vo. 1843. 5s.
5. History of the Almohades. Edited in Arabic by Dr. R. P. A. Dozy. 8vo. 1847. 10*s*. 6*d*.

Oriental Text Society—*continued.*

6. Sama Veda. Edited in Sanskrit by Rev. G. Stevenson. 8vo. 1843. 12*s.*
7. Dasa Kumara Charita. Edited in Sanskrit by Professor H. H. Wilson. 8vo. 1846. £1 4*s.*
8. Maha Vira Charita, or a History of Rama. A Sanskrit Play. Edited by F. H. Trithen. 8vo. 1848. 15*s.*
9. Mazhzan ul Asrar: The Treasury of Secrets. By Nizami. Edited in Persian by N. Bland. 4to. 1844. 10*s.* 6*d.*
10. Salaman-u-Ubsal; A Romance of Jami (Dshami). Edited in Persian by F. Falconer. 4to. 1843. 10*s.*
11. Mirkhond's History of the Atabeks. Edited in Persian by W. H. Morley. 8vo. 1850. 12*s.*
12. Tuhfat-ul-Ahrar; the Gift of the Noble. A Poem. By Jami (Dshami). Edited in Persian by F. Falconer. 4to. 1843. 10*s.*

Osburn.—The Monumental History of Egypt, as recorded on the Ruins of her Temples, Palaces, and Tombs. By William Osburn. Illustrated with Maps, Plates, etc. 2 vols. 8vo. pp. xii. and 461; vii. and 643, cloth. £2 2*s.*

Vol. I.—From the Colonization of the Valley to the Visit of the Patriarch Abram.
Vol. II.—From the Visit of Abram to the Exodus.

Palmer.—Egyptian Chronicles, with a harmony of Sacred and Egyptian Chronology, and an Appendix on Babylonian and Assyrian Antiquities. By William Palmer, M.A., and late Fellow of Magdalen College, Oxford. 2 vols., 8vo. cloth, pp. lxxiv. and 428, and viii. and 636. 1861. 12*s.*

Pand-Námah.—The Pand-Námah; or, Books of Counsels. By Ádarbád Máráspand. Translated from Pehlevi into Gujerathi, by Harbad Sheriarjee Dadabhoy. And from Gujerathi into English by the Rev. Shapurji Edalji. Fcap. 8vo. sewed. 1870. 6*d.*

Pandit's (A) Remarks on Professor Max Müller's Translation of the "Rig-Veda." Sanskrit and English. Fcap. 8vo. sewed. 1870. 6*d.*

Paspati.—Études sur les Tchinghianés (Gypsies) ou Bohémiens de l'Empire Ottoman. Par Alexandre G. Paspati, M.D. Large 8vo. sewed, pp. xii. and 652. Constantinople, 1871. 28*s.*

Patell.—Cowasjee Patell's Chronology, containing corresponding Dates of the different Eras used by Christians, Jews, Greeks, Hindús, Mohamedans, Parsees, Chinese, Japanese, etc. By Cowasjee Sorabjee Patell. 4to. pp. viii. and 184, cloth. 50*s.*

Pauthier.—Le Livre de Marco Polo, Citoyen de Vénise, Conseiller Privé et Commissaire Impérial de Khoubilaï-Khaán. Rédigé en français sous sa dictée en 1298 par Rusticien de Pise; Publié pour la première fois d'après trois manuscrits inédits de la Bibliothèque Impériale de Paris, présentant la rédaction primitive du Livre, revue par Marco Polo lui-même et donneé par lui, en 1307, à Thiébault de Cépoy, accompagnée des Variantes, de l'Explication des mots hors d'usage, et de commentaires géographiques et historiques, tirés des écrivains orientaux, principalement Chinois, avec une Carte générale de l'Asie par M. G. Pauthier. Two vols. roy. 8vo. pp. clvi. 832. With Map and View of Marco Polo's House at Venice. £1 8*s.*

Percy.—Bishop Percy's Folio Manuscripts—Ballads and Romances. Edited by John W. Hales, M.A., Fellow and late Assistant Tutor of Christ's College, Cambridge; and Frederick J. Furnivall, M.A., of Trinity Hall, Cambridge; assisted by Professor Child, of Harvard University, Cambridge, U.S.A., W. Chappell, Esq., etc. In 3 volumes. Vol. I., pp. 610; Vol. 2, pp. 681.; Vol. 3, pp. 640. Demy 8vo. half-bound, £4 4*s.* Extra demy 8vo. half-bound, on Whatman's ribbed paper, £6 6*s.* Extra royal 8vo., paper covers, on Whatman's best ribbed paper, £10 10*s.* Large 4to., paper covers, on Whatman's best ribbed paper, £12.

Perny.—DICTIONNAIRE FRANÇAIS-LATIN-CHINOIS DE LA LANGUE MANDARINE PARLÉE. Par PAUL PERNY. M.A., de la Congrégation des Missions Etrangères. 4to. pp. viii. 459, sewed. £2 2*s.*

Perny.—GRAMMAIRE PRATIQUE DE LA LANGUE MANDARINE PARLÉE. Par PAUL PERNY, M.A., de la Congrégation des Missions Etrangères. [*In the Press.*

Perny.—PROVERBES CHINOIS, RECUEILLIS ET MIS EN ORDRE. Par PAUL PERNY, M.A., de la Congrégation des Missions Etrangères. 12mo. pp. iv. 135. 3*s.*

Perrin.—ENGLISH-ZULU DICTIONARY. New Edition, revised by J. A. BRICKHILL, Interpreter to the Supreme Court of Natal. 12mo. pp. 226, cloth, Pietermaritzburg, 1865. 5*s.*

Philological Society.—PROPOSALS for the Publication of a NEW ENGLISH DICTIONARY. 8vo. pp. 32, sewed. 6*d.*

Pierce the Ploughman's Crede (about 1394 Anno Domini). Transcribed and Edited from the MS. of Trinity College, Cambridge, R. 3, 15. Collated with the MS. Bibl. Reg. 18. B. xvii. in the British Museum, and with the old Printed Text of 1553, to which is appended "God spede the Plough" (about 1500 Anno Domini), from the Lansdowne MS. 762. By the Rev. WALTER W. SKEAT, M.A., late Fellow of Christ's College, Cambridge. pp. xx. and 75, cloth. 1867. 2*s.* 6*d.*

Prakrita-Prakasa; or, The Prakrit Grammar of Vararuchi, with the Commentary (Manorama) of Bhamaha. The first complete edition of the Original Text with Various Readings from a Collation of Six Manuscripts in the Bodleian Library at Oxford, and the Libraries of the Royal Asiatic Society and the East India House; with copious Notes, an English Translation, and Index of Prakrit words, to which is prefixed an easy Introduction to Prakrit Grammar. By EDWARD BYLES COWELL, of Magdalen Hall, Oxford, Professor of Sanskrit at Cambridge. Second issue, with new Preface, and corrections. 8vo. pp. xxxii. and 204. 14*s.*

Priaulx.—QUÆSTIONES MOSAICÆ; or, the first part of the Book of Genesis compared with the remains of ancient religions. By OSMOND DE BEAUVOIR PRIAULX. 8vo. pp. viii. and 548, cloth. 12*s.*

Raghuvansa.—No. 1. (Cantos 1-3.) See under KALIDASA.

Raja-Niti.—A COLLECTION OF HINDU APOLOGUES, in the Braj Bháshá Language. Revised edition. With a Preface, Notes, and Supplementary Glossary. By FITZEDWARD HALL, Esq. 8vo. cloth, pp. 204. 21*s.*

Rámáyan of Válmiki.—Vols. I. and II. See under GRIFFITH.

Ram Jasan.—A SANSKRIT AND ENGLISH DICTIONARY. Being an Abridgment of Professor Wilson's Dictionary. With an Appendix explaining the use of Affixes in Sanskrit. By Pandit RAM JASAN, Queen's College, Benares. Published under the Patronage of the Government, N.W.P. Royal 8vo. cloth, pp. ii. and 707. 28*s.*

Ram Raz.—ESSAY on the ARCHITECTURE of the HINDUS. By RAM RAZ, Native Judge and Magistrate of Bangalore, Corresponding Member of the R.A.S. of Great Britain and Ireland. With 48 plates. 4to. pp. xiv. and 64, sewed. London, 1834. Original selling price, £1 11*s.* 6*d.*, reduced (for a short time) to 12*s.*

Rask.—A GRAMMAR OF THE ANGLO-SAXON TONGUE. From the Danish of Erasmus Rask, Professor of Literary History in, and Librarian to, the University of Copenhagen, etc. By BENJAMIN THORPE, Member of the Munich Royal Academy of Sciences, and of the Society of Netherlandish Literature, Leyden. Second edition, corrected and improved. 18mo. pp. 200, cloth. 5*s.* 6*d.*

Rawlinson.—A COMMENTARY ON THE CUNEIFORM INSCRIPTIONS OF BABYLONIA AND ASSYRIA, including Readings of the Inscription on the Nimrud Obelisk, and Brief Notice of the Ancient Kings of Nineveh and Babylon, Read before the Royal Asiatic Society, by Major H. C. RAWLINSON. 8vo., pp. 84, sewed. London, 1850. 2*s.* 6*d.*

Rawlinson.—OUTLINES OF ASSYRIAN HISTORY, from the Inscriptions of Nineveh. By Lieut. Col. RAWLINSON, C.B., followed by some Remarks by A. H. LAYARD, Esq., D.C.L. 8vo., pp. xliv., sewed. London, 1852. 1*s.*

Renan.—AN ESSAY ON THE AGE AND ANTIQUITY OF THE BOOK OF NABATHÆAN AGRICULTURE. To which is added an Inaugural Lecture on the Position of the Shemitic Nations in the History of Civilization. By M. ERNEST RENAN, Membre de l'Institut. Crown 8vo., pp. xvi. and 148, cloth. 3*s.* 6*d.*

Revue Celtique.—THE REVUE CELTIQUE, a Quarterly Magazine for Celtic Philology, Literature, and History. Edited with the assistance of the Chief Celtic Scholars of the British Islands and of the Continent, and Conducted by H. GAIDOZ. 8vo. Subscription, £1 per Volume.

Ridley.—KAMILAROI, DIPPIL, AND TURRUBUL. Languages Spoken by Australian Aborigines. By Rev. WM. RIDLEY, M.A., of the University of Sydney; Minister of the Presbyterian Church of New South Wales. Printed by authority. Small 4to. cloth, pp. vi. and 90. 30*s.*

Rig-Veda.—A NEW EDITION OF THE HYMNS OF THE RIG-VEDA IN THE SANHITÁ TEXT, without the Commentary of the Sâyana. Based upon the Editio princeps of MAX MÜLLER. Large 8vo. of about 800 pages. *See also under Max Müller.* [*In preparation.*

Rig-Veda-Sanhita: THE SACRED HYMNS OF THE BRAHMANS. Translated and explained by F. MAX MÜLLER, M.A., LL.D., Fellow of All Soul's College, Professor of Comparative Philology at Oxford, Foreign Member of the Institute of France, etc., etc. Vol. I. HYMNS TO THE MARUTS, OR THE STORM-GODS. 8vo. pp. clii. and 264. cloth. 1869. 12*s.* 6*d.*

Rig-Veda Sanhita.—A COLLECTION OF ANCIENT HINDU HYMNS. Constituting the First Ashtaka, or Book of the Rig-veda; the oldest authority for the religious and social institutions of the Hindus. Translated from the Original Sanskrit. By the late H. H. WILSON, M.A., F.R.S., etc. etc. etc. Second Edition, with a Postscript by Dr. FITZEDWARD HALL. Vol. I. 8vo. cloth, pp. lii. and 348, price 21*s.*

Rig-veda Sanhita.—A Collection of Ancient Hindu Hymns, constituting the Fifth to Eighth Ashtakas, or books of the Rig-Veda, the oldest Authority for the Religious and Social Institutions of the Hindus. Translated from the Original Sanskrit by the late HORACE HAYMAN WILSON, M.A., F.R.S., etc. Edited by E. B. COWELL, M.A., Principal of the Calcutta Sanskrit College. Vol. IV., 8vo., pp. 214, cloth. 14*s.*
A few copies of Vols. II. and III. still left. [*Vols. V. and VI. in the Press.*

Rudy.—THE CHINESE MANDARIN LANGUAGE, after Ollendorff's new method of learning languages. By CHARLES RUDY. [*In preparation.*

Sâma-Vidhâna-Brâhmana. With the Commentary of Sâyana. Edited, with Notes, Translation, and Index, by A. C. BURNELL, M.R.A.S., Madras Civil Service. In 1 vol. 8vo. [*In preparation.*

Sayce.—AN ASSYRIAN GRAMMAR. By the Rev. A. H. SAYCE, Queen's College, Oxford. Crown 8vo. [*In the Press.*

Schele de Vere.—STUDIES IN ENGLISH; or, Glimpses of the Inner Life of our Language. By M. SCHELE DE VERE, LL.D., Professor of Modern Languages in the University of Virginia. 8vo. cloth, pp. vi. and 365. 10*s.* 6*d.*

Schemeil.—EL MUBTAKER; or, First Born. (In Arabic, printed at Beyrout). Containing Five Comedies, called Comedies of Fiction, on Hopes and Judgments, in Twenty-six Poems of 1092 Verses, showing the Seven Stages of Life, from man's conception unto his death and burial. By EMIN IBRAHIM SCHEMEIL. In one volume, 4to. pp. 166, sewed. 1870. 5*s.*

Schlagintweit.—BUDDHISM IN TIBET. Illustrated by Literary Documents and Objects of Religious Worship. With an Account of the Buddhist Systems preceding it in India. By EMIL SCHLAGINTWEIT, LL.D. With a Folio Atlas of 20 Plates, and 20 Tables of Native Prints in the Text. Royal 8vo., pp. xxiv. and 404. £2 2*s.*

Schlagintweit.—GLOSSARY OF GEOGRAPHICAL TERMS FROM INDIA AND TIBET, with Native Transcription and Transliteration. By HERMANN DE SCHLAGINTWEIT. Forming, with a "Route Book of the Western Himalaya, Tibet, and Turkistan," the Third Volume of H., A., and R. DE SCHLAGINTWEIT'S "Results of a Scientific Mission to India and High Asia." With an Atlas in imperial folio, of Maps, Panoramas, and Views. Royal 4to., pp. xxiv. and 293. £4.

Schlottmann.—THE MONUMENT OF A VICTORY OF MESHA, King of the Moabites. A Contribution to Hebrew Archæology by Dr. KONSTANTIN SCHLOTTMANN, Professor of Theology at the University of Halle. Translated from the German. [*In the Press.*

Shápurjí Edaljí.—A GRAMMAR OF THE GUJARÁTÍ LANGUAGE. By SHÁPURJÍ EDALJÍ. Cloth, pp. 127. 10*s.* 6*d.*

Shápurjí Edaljí.—A DICTIONARY, GUJRATI AND ENGLISH. By SHÁPURJÍ EDALJÍ. Second Edition. Crown 8vo. cloth, pp. xxiv. and 874. 21*s.*

Sherring—THE SACRED CITY OF THE HINDUS. An Account of Benares in Ancient and Modern Times. By the Rev. M. A. SHERRING, M.A., LL.D.; and Prefaced with an Introduction by FITZEDWARD HALL, Esq., D.C.L. 8vo. cloth, pp. xxxvi. and 388, with numerous full-page illustrations. 21*s.*

Smith.—A VOCABULARY OF PROPER NAMES IN CHINESE AND ENGLISH. of Places, Persons, Tribes, and Sects, in China, Japan, Corea, Assam, Siam, Burmah, The Straits, and adjacent Countries. By F. PORTER SMITH, M.B., China. 4to. half-bound, pp. vi., 72, and x. 1870. 10*s.* 6*d.*

Smith.—CONTRIBUTIONS TOWARDS THE MATERIA MEDICA AND NATURAL HISTORY OF CHINA. For the use of Medical Missionaries and Native Medical Students. By F. PORTER SMITH, M.B. London, Medical Missionary in Central China. Imp. 4to. cloth, pp. viii. and 240. 1870. £1 1*s.*

Sophocles.—A GLOSSARY OF LATER AND BYZANTINE GREEK. By E. A. SOPHOCLES. 4to., pp. iv. and 624, cloth. £2 2*s.*

Sophocles.—ROMAIC OR MODERN GREEK GRAMMAR. By E. A. SOPHOCLES. 8vo. pp. xxviii. and 196. 7*s.* 6*d.*

Sophocles.—GREEK LEXICON OF THE ROMAN AND BYZANTINE PERIODS (from B.C. 146 to A.D. 1100). By E. A. SOPHOCLES. Imp. 8vo. pp. xvi. 1188, cloth. 1870. £2 8*s.*

Steele.—AN EASTERN LOVE STORY. KUSA JÁTAKAYA: a Buddhistic Legendary Poem, with other Stories. By THOMAS STEELE, Ceylon Civil Service. Crown 8vo. cloth, pp. xii. and 260. 1871. 6*s.*

Stratmann.—A DICTIONARY OF THE ENGLISH LANGUAGE. Compiled from the writings of the XIIIth, XIVth, and XVth centuries. By FRANCIS HENRY STRATMANN. Second Edition. Part I. Small 4to., pp. 160, price 10*s.* 6*d.*

Stratmann.—AN OLD ENGLISH POEM OF THE OWL AND THE NIGHTINGALE. Edited by FRANCIS HENRY STRATMANN. 8vo. cloth, pp. 60. 3*s.*

Surya-Siddhanta (Translation of the).—A TEXT BOOK OF HINDU ASTRONOMY, with Notes and Appendix, &c. By Rev. EBENEZER BURGESS. 8vo. pp. iv. and 354, boards. 15*s.*

Syed Ahmed.—A SERIES OF ESSAYS ON THE LIFE OF MOHAMMED, and Subjects subsidiary thereto. By SYED AHMED KHAN BAHADOR, C.S.I., Author of the "Mohammedan Commentary on the Holy Bible," Honorary Member of the Royal Asiatic Society, and Life Honorary Secretary to the Allygurh Scientific Society. 8vo. pp. 532, with 4 Genealogical Tables, 2 Maps, and a Coloured Plate, handsomely bound in cloth. 30*s.*

Tabari.—CHRONIQUE DE ABOU-DJAFAR-MOHAMMED-BEN-DJARIR-BEN-YEZID. Traduite par Monsieur HERMANN ZOTENBERG. Vol. I, 8vo. pp. 608. Vol. II, 8vo. pp. ii. and 252, sewed. 7*s.* 6*d.* each. (*To be completed in Four Volumes.*)

Táittiríya-Prâtiçâkhya.—See under WHITNEY.

The Boke of Nurture. By JOHN RUSSELL, about 1460–1470 Anno Domini. The Boke of Keruynge. By WYNKYN DE WORDE, Anno Domini 1513. The Boke of Nurture. By HUGH RHODES, Anno Domini 1577. Edited from the Originals in the British Museum Library, by FREDERICK J. FURNIVALL, M.A., Trinity Hall, Cambridge, Member of Council of the Philological and Early English Text Societies. 4to. half-morocco, gilt top, pp. xix. and 146, 28, xxviii. and 56. 1867. 1*l.* 11*s.* 6*d.*

The Vision of William concerning Piers Plowman, together with Vita de Dowel, Dobet et Dobest, secundum wit et resoun. By WILLIAM LANGLAND (about 1362-1380 anno domini). Edited from numerous Manuscripts, with Prefaces, Notes, and a Glossary. By the Rev. WALTER W. SKEAT M.A. pp. xliv. and 158, cloth, 1867. Vernon A. Text; Text 7*s.* 6*d.*

Thomas.—EARLY SASSANIAN INSCRIPTIONS, SEALS AND COINS, illustrating the Early History of the Sassanian Dynasty, containing Proclamations of Ardeshir Babek, Sapor I., and his Successors. With a Critical Examination and Explanation of the Celebrated Inscription in the Hájiábad Cave, demonstrating that Sapor, the Conqueror of Valerian, was a Professing Christian. By EDWARD THOMAS, Esq. Illustrated. 8vo. cloth, pp. 148. 7*s.* 6*d.*

Thomas.—THE CHRONICLES OF THE PATHÁN KINGS OF DEHLI. Illustrated by Coins, Inscriptions, and other Antiquarian Remains. By EDWARD THOMAS, F.R.A.S., late of the East India Company's Bengal Civil Service. With numerous Copperplates and Woodcuts. Demy 8vo. cloth, pp. xxiv. and 467. 1871. 28*s.*

Thomas.—THE REVENUE RESOURCES OF THE MUGHAL EMPIRE IN INDIA, from A.D. 1593 to A.D. 1707. A Supplement to "The Chronicles of the Pathán Kings of Delhi." By EDWARD THOMAS, F.R.S., late of the East India Company's Bengal Civil Service. Demy 8vo., pp. 60, cloth. 3*s.* 6*d.*

Thomas.—ESSAYS ON INDIAN ANTIQUITIES: following up the Discoveries of James Prinsep, with specimens of his Engravings, and selections from his Useful Tables, and embodying the most recent investigations into the History, Palæography, and Numismatics of Ancient India. By EDWARD THOMAS, late of the East India Company's Bengal Civil Service. In 2 vols. 8vo., profusely illustrated. [*In preparation.*

Thomas.—THE THEORY AND PRACTICE OF CREOLE GRAMMAR. By J. J. THOMAS. Port of Spain (Trinidad), 1869. One vol. 8vo. boards, pp. viii. and 135. 12*s.*

Thonissen.—ÉTUDES SUR L'HISTOIRE DU DROIT CRIMINEL DES PEUPLES Anciens (Inde Brahmanique, E'gypte, Judée), par J. J. THONISSEN, Professeur à l'Université Catholique de Louvain, Membre de l'Academie Royale de Belgique. 2 vols. 8vo. pp. xvi. 248, 320, sewed. 1869. 12*s.*

Thorpe.—DIPLOMATARIUM ANGLICUM ÆVI SAXONICI. A Collection of English Charters, from the reign of King Æthelberht of Kent, A.D., DCV., to that of William the Conqueror. Containing: I. Miscellaneous Charters. II. Wills. III. Guilds. IV. Manumissions and Acquittances. With a Translation of the Anglo-Saxon. By the late BENJAMIN THORPE, Member of the Royal Academy of Sciences at Munich, and of the Society of Netherlandish Literature at Leyden. 8vo. pp. xlii. and 682, cloth. 1865. £1 1*s.*

Tindall.—A GRAMMAR AND VOCABULARY OF THE NAMAQUA-HOTTENTOT LANGUAGE. By HENRY TINDALL, Wesleyan Missionary. 8vo. pp. 124, sewed. 6*s.*

Van der Tuuk.—OUTLINES OF A GRAMMAR OF THE MALAGASY LANGUAGE By H. N. VAN DER TUUK. 8vo., pp. 28, sewed. 1*s.*

Van der Tuuk.—SHORT ACCOUNT OF THE MALAY MANUSCRIPTS BELONGING TO THE ROYAL ASIATIC SOCIETY. By H. N. VAN DER TUUK. 8vo., pp. 52. 2*s.* 6*d.*

Vishnu-Purana (The); a System of Hindu Mythology and Tradition. Translated from the original Sanskrit, and Illustrated by Notes derived chiefly from other Purâṇas. By the late H. H. WILSON, M.A., F.R.S., Boden Professor of Sanskrit in the University of Oxford, etc., etc. Edited by FITZEDWARD HALL. In 6 vols. 8vo. Vol. I. pp. cxl. and 200; Vol. II. pp. 343; Vol. III. pp. 348; Vol. IV. pp. 346, cloth; Vol. V. pp. 392, cloth. 10*s.* 6*d.* each.

Vullers.—A GRAMMAR OF THE PERSIAN LANGUAGE. By J. A. VULLERS, Professor of Oriental Languages in the University of Giessen. 8vo. [*In the Press.*

Wade.—YÜ-YEN TZŬ-ERH CHI. A progressive course designed to assist the Student of Colloquial Chinese, as spoken in the Capital and the Metropolitan Department. In eight parts, with Key, Syllabary, and Writing Exercises. By THOMAS FRANCIS WADE, C.B., Secretary to Her Britannic Majesty's Legation, Peking. 3 vols. 4to. Progressive Course, pp. xx. 296 and 16; Syllabary, pp. 126 and 36; Writing Exercises, pp. 48; Key, pp. 174 and 140, sewed. £4.

Wade.—WÊN-CHIEN TZŬ-ERH CHI. A series of papers selected as specimens of documentary Chinese, designed to assist Students of the language, as written by the officials of China. In sixteen parts, with Key. Vol. I. By THOMAS FRANCIS WADE, C.B., Secretary to Her Britannic Majesty's Legation at Peking. 4to., half-cloth, pp. xii. and 455; and iv., 72, and 52. £1 16*s.*

Wake.—CHAPTERS ON MAN. With the Outlines of a Science of comparative Psychology. By C. STANILAND WAKE, Fellow of the Anthropological Society of London. Crown 8vo. pp. viii. and 344, cloth. 7*s.* 6*d.*

Watson.—INDEX TO THE NATIVE AND SCIENTIFIC NAMES OF INDIAN AND OTHER EASTERN ECONOMIC PLANTS AND PRODUCTS, originally prepared under the authority of the Secretary of State for India in Council. By JOHN FORBES WATSON, M.A., M.D., F.L.S., F.R.A.S., etc., Reporter on the Products of India. Imperial 8vo., cloth, pp. 650. £1 11*s.* 6*d.*

Watts.—ESSAYS ON LANGUAGE AND LITERATURE. By THOMAS WATTS, late of the British Museum. Reprinted, with Alterations and Additions, from the Transactions of the Philological Society, and elsewhere. In 1 vol. 8vo. [*In preparation.*

Webster.—AN INTRODUCTORY ESSAY TO THE SCIENCE OF COMPARATIVE THEOLOGY; with a Tabular Synopsis of Scientific Religion. By EDWARD WEBSTER, of Ealing, Middlesex. Read in an abbreviated form as a Lecture to a public audience at Ealing, on the 3rd of January, 1870, and to an evening congregation at South Place Chapel, Finsbury Square, London, on the 27th of February, 1870. 8vo. pp. 28, sewed. 1870. 1*s.*

Wedgwood.—A DICTIONARY OF THE ENGLISH LANGUAGE. By HENSLEIGH WEDGWOOD, M.A. late Fellow of Christ's College, Cambridge. Vol. I. (A to D) 8vo., pp. xxiv. 508, cloth, 14*s.*; Vol. II. (E to P) 8vo. pp. 578, cloth, 14*s.*; Vol. III., Part I. (Q to Sy), 8vo. pp. 366, 10*s.* 6*d.*; Vol. III. Part II. (T to W) 8vo. pp. 200, 5*s.* 6*d.* completing the Work. Price of the complete work, £2 4*s.*

"Dictionaries are a class of books not usually esteemed light reading; but no intelligent man were to be pitied who should find himself shut up on a rainy day in a lonely house in the dreariest part of Salisbury Plain, with no other means of recreation than that which Mr. Wedgwood's Dictionary of Etymology could afford him. He would read it through from cover to cover at a sitting, and only regret that he had not the second volume to begin upon forthwith. It is a very able book, of great research, full of delightful surprises, a repertory of the fairy tales of linguistic science."—*Spectator.*

Wedgwood.—A DICTIONARY OF ENGLISH ETYMOLOGY. By HENSLEIGH WEDGWOOD. Second Edition, thoroughly revised and corrected by the Author, and extended to the Classical Roots of the Language. With an Introduction on the Formation of Language. Imperial 8vo., about 800 pages, double column. In Five Monthly Parts, of 160 pages. Price 5*s.* each; or complete in one volume, cl., price 25*s.*

Wedgwood.—ON THE ORIGIN OF LANGUAGE. By HENSLEIGH WEDGWOOD, late Fellow of Christ's College, Cambridge. Fcap. 8vo. pp. 172, cloth. 3*s.* 6*d.*

Wékey.—A GRAMMAR OF THE HUNGARIAN LANGUAGE, with appropriate Exercises, a Copious Vocabulary, and Specimens of Hungarian Poetry. By SIGISMUND WÉKEY, late Aide-de-Camp to Kossuth. 12mo., pp. xii. and 150, sewed. 4*s.* 6*d.*

West and Bühler.—DIGEST OF HINDU LAW, from the Replies of the Shastris in the several Courts of the Bombay Presidency. With an Introduction, Notes, and Appendix. Edited by RAYMOND WEST and JOHANN GEORG BÜHLER. Vol. I. 8vo. cloth. £3 3*s*. Vol. II. 8vo. pp. v. 118, cloth. 12*s*.

Wheeler.—THE HISTORY OF INDIA FROM THE EARLIEST AGES. By J. TALBOYS WHEELER, Assistant Secretary to the Government of India in the Foreign Department, Secretary to the Indian Record Commission, author of "The Geography of Herodotus," etc. etc.

Vol. I., The Vedic Period and the Maha Bharata. 8vo. cloth, pp. lxxv. and 576. 18*s*.

Vol. II., The Ramayana and the Brahmanic Period. 8vo. cloth, pp. lxxxviii. and 680, with 2 Maps. 21*s*.

Wheeler.—JOURNAL OF A VOYAGE UP THE IRRAWADDY TO MANDALAY AND BHAMO. By J. TALBOYS WHEELER. 8vo. pp. 104, sewed. 1871. 3*s*. 6*d*.

Whitney.—ATHARVA VEDA PRÁTIÇÁKHYA; or, Çáunakíyá Caturádhyáyiká (The). Text, Translation, and Notes. By WILLIAM D. WHITNEY, Professor of Sanskrit in Yale College. 8vo. pp. 286, boards. 12*s*.

Whitney.—LANGUAGE AND THE STUDY OF LANGUAGE: Twelve Lectures on the Principles of Linguistic Science. By WILLIAM DWIGHT WHITNEY, Professor of Sanskrit, etc., in Yale College. Third Edition, augmented by an Analysis. Crown 8vo. cloth, pp. xii. and 504. 10*s*. 6*d*.

Whitney.—TÁITTIRÍYA-PRÁTIÇÁKHYA, with its Commentary, the Tribháshyaratna: Text, Translation, and Notes. By W. D. WHITNEY, Prof. of Sanskrit in Yale College, New Haven. 8vo. pp. 469. 1871. 25*s*.

Wilkins.—THE BHAGAVAT-GEETA; or, Dialogues of Kreeshna and Arjoon. Translated by CHAS. WILKINS. A faithful reprint of the now very scarce Original London Edition of 1785, made at the Bradsheet Press, New York. In one vol. 8vo. Beautifully printed with old face type on laid paper. 261 copies were produced of this edition, of which only a few now remain. 12*s*.

Williams.—FIRST LESSONS IN THE MAORI LANGUAGE, with a Short Vocabulary. By W. L. WILLIAMS, B.A. Square 8vo., pp. 80, cloth, London, 1862. 10*s*.

Williams.—LEXICON CORNU-BRITANNICUM. A Dictionary of the Ancient Celtic Language of Cornwall, in which the words are elucidated by copious examples from the Cornish works now remaining, with translations in English. The synonyms are also given in the cognate dialects of Welsh, Armoric, Irish, Gaelic, and Manx, showing at one view the connexion between them. By the Rev. ROBERT WILLIAMS, M.A., Christ Church, Oxford, Parish Curate of Llangadwaladr and Rhydycroesan, Denbighshire. Sewed. 3 parts, pp. 400. £2 5*s*.

Williams.—A DICTIONARY, ENGLISH AND SANSCRIT. By MONIER WILLIAMS, M.A. Published under the Patronage of the Honourable East India Company. 4to. pp. xii. 862, cloth. London, 1855. £3 3*s*.

Wilson.—Works of the late HORACE HAYMAN WILSON, M.A., F.R.S., Member of the Royal Asiatic Societies of Calcutta and Paris, and of the Oriental Society of Germany, etc., and Boden Professor of Sanskrit in the University of Oxford.

Vols I. and II. ESSAYS AND LECTURES chiefly on the Religion of the Hindus, by the late H. H. WILSON, M.A., F.R.S., etc. Collected and edited by Dr. REINHOLD ROST. 2 vols. cloth, pp. xiii. and 399, vi. and 416. 21*s*.

Vols. III, IV. and V. ESSAYS ANALYTICAL, CRITICAL, AND PHILOLOGICAL, ON SUBJECTS CONNECTED WITH SANSKRIT LITERATURE. Collected and Edited by Dr. REINHOLD ROST. 3 vols. 8vo. pp. 408, 406, and 390, cloth. Price 36*s*.

Vols. VI., VII., VIII, IX. and X. VISHNU PURÁNÁ, A SYSTEM OF HINDU MYTHOLOGY AND TRADITION. Translated from the original Sanskrit, and Illustrated by Notes derived chiefly from other Puráṇás. By the late H. H. WILSON, Boden Professor of Sanskrit in the University of Oxford, etc., etc. Edited by FITZEDWARD HALL, M.A., D.C.L., Oxon. Vols. I. to V. 8vo., pp. cxl. and 200; 344; 344; 346, cloth. 2*l.* 12*s.* 6*d.*

Vols. XI. and XII. SELECT SPECIMENS OF THE THEATRE OF THE HINDUS. Translated from the Original Sanskrit. By the late HORACE HAYMAN WILSON, M.A., F.R.S. Third corrected Edition. 2 vols. 8vo. pp. lxi. and 384; and iv. and 418, cloth. 21*s.*

Wilson.—SELECT SPECIMENS OF THE THEATRE OF THE HINDUS. Translated from the Original Sanskrit. By the late HORACE HAYMAN WILSON, M.A., F.R.S. Third corrected edition. 2 vols. 8vo., pp. lxxi. and 384; iv. and 418, cloth. 21*s.*

CONTENTS.

Vol. I.—Preface—Treatise on the Dramatic System of the Hindus—Dramas translated from the Original Sanskrit—The Mrichchakati, or the Toy Cart—Vikram aand Urvasi, or the Hero and the Nymph—Uttara Ráma Charitra, or continuation of the History of Ráma.

Vol. II.—Dramas translated from the Original Sanskrit—Maláti and Mádhava, or the Stolen Marriage—Mudrá Rakshasa, or the Signet of the Minister—Ratnávalí, or the Necklace—Appendix, containing short accounts of different Dramas.

Wilson.—THE PRESENT STATE OF THE CULTIVATION OF ORIENTAL LITERATURE. A Lecture delivered at the Meeting of the Royal Asiatic Society. By the Director, Professor H. H. WILSON. 8vo., pp. 26, sewed. London, 1852. 6*d.*

Wise.—COMMENTARY ON THE HINDU SYSTEM OF MEDICINE. By T. A. WISE, M.D., Bengal Medical Service. 8vo., pp. xx. and 432, cloth. 7*s.* 6*d.*

Wright.—THE HOMES OF OTHER DAYS. A History of Domestic Manners and Sentiments during the Middle Ages. By THOMAS WRIGHT, Esq., M.A., F.S.A. With Illustrations from the Illuminations in Contemporary Manuscripts and other Sources. Drawn and Engraved by F. W. FAIRHOLT, Esq., F.S.A. 1 vol. medium 8vo., 350 Woodcuts, pp. xv. and 512, handsomely bound in cloth. 21*s.*

Wright.—A VOLUME OF VOCABULARIES, illustrating the Condition and Manners of our Forefathers, as well as the History of the forms of Elementary Education, and of the Languages Spoken in this Island from the Tenth Century to the Fifteenth. Edited by THOMAS WRIGHT, Esq., M.A., F.S.A., &c., &c.

[*In the Press.*

Wright.—THE CELT, THE ROMAN, AND THE SAXON; a History of the Early Inhabitants of Britain down to the Conversion of the Anglo-Saxons to Christianity. Illustrated by the Ancient Remains brought to light by Recent Research. By THOMAS WRIGHT, Esq., M.A., F.S.A., etc., etc. Third Corrected and Enlarged Edition. [*In the Press.*

Wylie.—NOTES ON CHINESE LITERATURE; with introductory Remarks on the Progressive Advancement of the Art; and a list of translations from the Chinese, into various European Languages. By A. WYLIE, Agent of the British and Foreign Bible Society in China. 4to. pp. 296, cloth. Price, 1*l.* 16*s.*

Yates.—A BENGÁLÍ GRAMMAR: By the late Rev. W. YATES, D.D. Reprinted, with improvements, from his Introduction to the Bengálí Language, Edited by I. WENGER. Fcap. 8vo., pp. iv. and 150, bds. Calcutta, 1864. 3*s.* 6*d.*

STEPHEN AUSTIN AND SONS, PRINTERS, HERTFORD.